MW01490509

Why We Climb

A Dirtbag's Quest for Vertical Reason

Why We Climb

A Dirtbag's Quest for Vertical Reason

By John Burgman

Published by Ground Up Publishing, LLC

Asheville, NC 28806

www.grounduppublishing.com

Copyright © 2015 by John Andrew Burgman

© 2015 Foreword by Arno Ilgner

© 1986 Text from *Moments of Doubt* by David Roberts reprinted with permission of the publisher, Mountaineers Books, Seattle.

© 1994 Text from *Camp 4* by Steve Roper reprinted with permission of the publisher, Mountaineers Books, Seattle.

Brigit Pegeen Kelly, "Pipistrelles" from *Song*. © 1995 by Brigit Pegeen Kelly. Reprinted with the permission of The Permissions Company, Inc., on behalf of BOA Editions, Ltd., www.boaeditions.org.

Layout and illustration by Mike Reardon of Ground Up Publishing, LLC.

Cover photo by Robert Miramontes

Back cover photo by Photobac

ISBN-10: 0692427902

ISBN-13: 978-0-692-42790-3

All photographs reprinted with permission. © belongs to the respective photographers or rights owners, and is attributed accordingly throughout the text.

All rights reserved. No part of this book may be rewritten or transmitted without pre written consent of the author or publisher, except in the case of brief quotes. Climbing is an inherently dangerous undertaking. In no way can the author or publisher be held responsible from injury or death that was a result of the use of this book.

This book is dedicated to

ANY CLIMBER WHO HAS EVER WONDERED WHY

www.GroundUpPublishing.com

Contents

Foreword

I'm selfish! I'm selfish because I engage in a pointless activity like climbing. What could be more pointless than searching for a difficult way to a summit? There are easier ways to get to the top, such as taking a helicopter. And, there are unselfish things we could do with our time. We could solve pressing global environmental issues or spend more time spreading goodwill. Climbing is selfish and pointless!

But, climbing challenges us too. It connects us in a primal way—touching, pulling, moving—to an activity that we chose. There's something important about being challenged. And, there's something important about being challenged in a way that we choose to be challenged. Choice gives us freedom to live, to live the kind of lives we want to live.

What's wrong with doing something that's selfish, anyway? Do we really need a reason to justify what we do with our time? The question, "Why do we climb?" points to our motivation, toward our search for meaning and purpose. We want to feel as if we count, that we matter. We want to feel alive, engaged in life as an active participant, not as a bystander. Climbing, even though it's selfish and pointless, gives us that.

Could being selfish about our climbing actually make us better people? And then, because we're better, give us power to be more effective in dealing with global issues or be able to spread goodwill? In other words, is it possible to be selfish about our climbing, in order to be unselfish with others?

John Burgman helps us dig into these issues. He cites climbers from Udo Neumann, with his understanding of competition climbing, to Chris Sharma, living out his life's purpose. He cites David Roberts, author of *Moments of Doubt*, noting that there's something within climbing that takes hold of us and begs us to answer fundamental questions. Such questions can clarify doubts and give us clear vision.

Life, engagement, meaning, purpose...all occur in the present moment. We can think about our past achievements, or about our dreams and future goals, but it's in the present that we live and climb. What motivation helps us be present? Is it the desire to achieve goals, or is it the passion of casting away those goals? Or is it a mix of both? Why, why, why...

What is pointless from one person's perspective is meaningful from the perspective of someone else. We all live our lives from our own perspectives. The choice is up to us to determine what is pointless or selfish, what is meaningful and what is not, how we can best add value or what limits our ability to add value. We must make those choices.

For me, to borrow a phrase from Chris Bonington, I chose to climb. I don't care if climbing is selfish or pointless. Climbing gives me meaning and purpose, a vision for my life. It allows me to sink to a primal level, to touch, to pull and move, in a medium I chose: rock. I like that feeling. So, I'll continue to do it.

—Arno Ilgner, author of *The Rock Warrior's Way*
La Vergne, Tennessee 2014

Preface

Years ago, while struggling to make ends meet as a freelance journalist in New York City, I took a job at a sprawling bookstore in Brooklyn. Part of the job, of course, entailed frequently re shelving books and magazines that customers had left strewn about the floor, discarded and abandoned on the carpet along with empty paper coffee cups, partially-eaten cookies, newspapers and other remnants of bookstore lounging. It was while doing such routine re-shelving one summer night that I came across a book titled *Why We Run*, by Bernd Heinrich. The book, as was explained on the back of its cover, was an exploration into the biological and anthropological underpinnings of jogging, racing, marathoning and human athletic endurance. I was immediately intrigued.

I bought the book, read it on the subway, and learned that the process of running has roots far deeper in human biological precondition and compulsion than I had ever imagined.

Years later, now far removed from my job at the bookstore and those salad days in New York City, one particular point lingers in my mind, and honestly it has gnawed at me for a long time. While I enjoyed Heinrich's book, and while I try to jog for exercise on a regular basis, I have long considered myself a climber as much as a runner.

I have plenty of friends who treat their daily jogs with the meticulous attention and conscientiousness of scientists. They wear heart rate monitors as they calculate their running tempo paces down to the minute or even down to the second, have the supinations or pronations of their feet digitally analyzed, spend hundreds of dollars every year on equipment like technical shoes and clothing (this, I admit, is a trait that runners readily share with climbers), and travel the country—or world—for the purpose of running marathons in far-flung cities. My friends' interest in running is an obsession and, as a result, a book like Heinrich's reaffirms that they have tapped into some primordial essence of mankind with their mania. *Man was designed to run*, and my friends are certainly following the blueprint, fulfilling a purpose.

But that same natural ease that my marathoning friends feel when racing on an open expanse of paved road, I feel when I am on vertical rock or even an indoor climbing wall, arms and legs splayed in counterbalance on the stone or the holds, fingers tightly grasping little pockets far above the earth. In a way, being in such contorted positions feels as intuitive to me as running, as normal as other physiological mechanics. In fact, for as long as I can remember, I have been drawn to climbing things—trees, big rocks, loft ceilings, bridges, scaffolding, stone siding of houses, whichever structure happened to be closest at hand.

Moreover, after spending a long time among various communities of climbers and outdoorsmen—both in the United States and internationally—I know that there are many other people who feel a similar kinship with the act of climbing, and there exits an entire subculture of individuals who feel equally compelled to move vertically. In light of all that, perhaps there is an instinctual element to it all also.

If nothing else, my love of being on the rocks, along with books like Heinrich's, has caused me to think of my outdoor pursuits in a grander context. After many hours of research and climbing, I believe that climbing has anthropological and evolutionary underpinnings as well.

Above all else, I rock climb because it is fun, and this book shouldn't be seen as a deranged manifesto proclaiming that mankind has taken a cultural misstep, that we are really meant to be living on precarious mountain ledges, crimping miniscule handholds 5,000 feet above valley floors instead of strutting bipedally on sidewalks, driving cars and constructing cul-de-sac houses on the quite-comfortable earthy ground.

Nor am I necessarily arguing that climbing is more or less of an instinctual action than is running, as such a comparison is useless. As you'll see later in the book, it is precisely the fact that man has so many diverse actions and capabilities in his repertoire—rather than relying solely on one such as running or swimming or climbing—that has contributed to his flourishing.

But we are descended from climbers. We are apes, and we are from apes—or at least a common ancestor of apes. We evolved from animals quite comfortable in a vertical world. And just like man's contemporary affinity for running might stem from his very primordial imperatives to chase and hunt game or flee swiftly from danger, is it possible that a contemporary affinity for climbing draws from the primordial inclination to climb as well?

On the surface, it might seem like the only ones who would consider that mankind has an affinity for climbing would be climbers themselves. After all, climbers tend to be superfluous in their praise of the sport, of both its virtues and its lifestyle. Yet, there are plenty of people in the world who would never climb a high rock, even if you offered them a stack of money of equal proportion.

That's a fair point, but the same could be said for running; to some people, the mechanics of jogging feel so awkward or painful that they either never exercise, or hopefully find other athletic avenues for healthy living like stationary bicycling or yoga. If one doesn't begin a long-term running routine with the proper planning, precautions and balance of rest, he'll be doomed to injury. In that case, the act of running would feel anything but intuitive.

Climbing has a similar entry portal. I'd be willing to bet that some people who scoff at the notion of mankind having an inborn affinity for climbing probably do so because they immediately envision a lone figure hanging from a dangerous, windswept precipice with one hand, *Cliffhanger*-style, or they drum up mental images of someone like Alex Honnold, a world-class free solo climber, scaling the peaks of Yosemite thousands of feet from the ground without the safety protection of ropes or a harness—a situation in which falling or slipping from the rock means near-certain death.

But those are the extremes of the climbing craft, and the disconnect comes because naysayers are focusing on the fantastic feats and the maximal panorama of the sport, rather than the mechanics.

To put it another way, I don't know if I really felt any affinity for running, in Heinrich's anthropological sense, when I watched running legend Haile Gebrselassie win the Olympic 10,000 meter race, or when I watched Usain Bolt break the world record for the 100 meter sprint. I just felt, well, impressed—and completely inadequate. But hone in on the organic mechanisms involved, explain to me running with regards to the leg muscles and the hip bones being ideally shaped for quick locomotion, the forefoot being designed to absorb significant downward impact, and I'm more swayed.

It's worth noting that a newborn infant, in the progressing stages of body mechanics and movement, gravitates to climbing before he learns to move on his feet. The old adage—*you must learn to walk before you can run*—could be amended with: *you must learn to climb before you can walk.* As one of the many science books I found throughout my research notes, "In the embryo, both the arms and legs develop rather late, with the lower limbs relatively inconspicuous, even for some time after birth, while the arms and hands are comparatively strong in the newborn."

The book you are now holding, or more particularly the summer recounted within it, was my modest attempt to shine some light on the different facets of the rock climbing experience—the physical, mental, liturgical, spiritual and competitive—and through that illumination, examine how the particular aspects play a part in the larger climbing craft, and how the origins of a given aspect might lie in our collective prehistoric past. I also draw from my own climbing experiences, in order to place it all in the context of my own life, upon which climbing has had a great positive impact. The book was never intended to be the discovery of a singular answer to broad inquiry. Rather, the narrative was—and remains—an earnest exploration into a complex and timeless question.

I wrote this book because compartmentalizing climbing in the context of my life, considering climbing to be mere recreation, does a disservice to the significant moments I have experienced and the wonderful people I have met because of the sport. If there is anyone reading this book who thinks that I'm making climbing out to be of larger importance than it actually is, I would encourage the skeptical reader to find a pristine mountainside in a beautiful wilderness on a crystalline morning, tie into a rope with a willing and knowledgeable partner, and give climbing a shot. See if it stirs the human spirit the way it has for me and for generations of others since the beginning of mankind.

A room with a view within Yosemite National Park
Photo: Greg Epperson/ Shutterstock

1 | Born to climb

One summer, after finishing up a handful of writing projects and spending my last dime on a few work-related trips in Asia that ultimately didn't amount to much writing (and subsequently didn't amount to any money or publishing payoff), I suddenly found myself with a substantial chunk of free time on my hands and a summer in which to rock climb as long and as hard as the daylight hours would allow. I was scheduled to start teaching a few classes at a university in the fall, nearly three months away, but aside from that commitment, I actively chose to restructure my life around climbing. It was an activity I had neglected from time to time over the years, but never lost sight of or lacked enthusiasm for. If anything, the times in my life when I hadn't climbed with the frequency I would have liked had made me long for climbing even more—to the point where I used to wake up an hour early on weekdays, eschew the headlines of the day, and instead read *Urban Climber, Rock & Ice, Outside* and *Climbing* magazines with my morning coffee before heading off to my office in New York City to start the daily grind.

So, when I finally had the good fortune of being able to jam-pack my summer days with every facet of the climbing craft—actually climbing and reading the magazines, and also studying the heritage of the sport and trying out new gear when I could afford it, talking to old-time climbers for hours on end—it felt almost as if I was being introduced to climbing for the first time. Being something of a born-again climber, this second coming prompted me to wonder about the magnificent pursuit in ways that I had largely taken for granted in the past. I had since left the tedium of the office, and the United States altogether, and moved to South Korea, a breathtaking peninsular country nestled between China and Japan, in which Buddhism is the predominant religion, bustling metropolises are juxtaposed with rice fields and rolling hills in the countryside, elaborate spicy meals and boisterous alcohol consumption are ingrained in the culture, and threats from the isolated neighboring enigma of North Korea are a common occurrence. Additionally, South Korea has a ghastly underrated climbing tradition, not to mention a mountainous geography that gives famous American climbing regions a run for their money. Best of all, given the circumstances, I was allowed to be a dirtbag there, mostly broke and untethered by ambitions beyond exploring the outdoors. Essentially, I was free to be free.

I had also made friends in South Korea's international climbing community, which stemmed from the capital city, Seoul, being a hub for world business. I had met climbers from China, Germany, England, Russia, Australia, Indonesia and New Zealand, and it fascinated me to hear their climbing points of reference. As a longtime bouldering fanatic, when I thought of climbing, my mind went instantly to Camp 4 in Yosemite, or the orbiculate rocks of Bishop, California, or Hueco Tanks outside of El Paso, Texas. But the European climbers, of course, talked of the Alps, or of Frankenjura in Germany, or of the picturesque cliffs of Mallorca, Spain. And my Korean friends raved about *Bukhan-san*, translated as *The Mountain to the North of the Han River*, in Seoul.

In the span of a few weeks, after regaling together over many beers in local Korean bars, my climbing consciousness was expanded by an exponential degree. In a way, it was the type of cross-cultural pollination I had been seeking during all those early mornings with my coffee and climbing magazines in New York City years ago.

I had also learned a fascinating truth about rock climbing: Despite its global appeal, climbing maintains a very communal aura, for ultimately getting on a rock in Asia is no different than getting on a rock in Red River Gorge, Kentucky. Sure, there are cultural differences and potentially thousands of miles between any two given crags, but there exists a sameness among the ragtag clan of climbers that frequent them. As an example, at the time that my full summer of climbing captivation began, I was a dirtbag writer from the Midwest, while the Korean owner of the indoor climbing gym down the street from my apartment in Seoul was a former architect turned full-time route-setter. Our upbringings and our points of cultural reference couldn't have been more different. Yet, I felt immediate camaraderie with him because all both of us wanted to do was fill our days with climbing.

I was so psyched for the yawning months of climbing laying ahead that I almost didn't know where to begin. But I figured that getting outdoors seemed like a good idea. After a little researching on the Internet, I found directions to an outdoor wall in a nearby city that was free to the public. I bought a train ticket and packed my chalk bag and climbing shoes, in full optimism that the wall would be as vast and inviting as the online post had made it seem. I was also optimistic that somebody there might be able to trade a belay or two with me, and that we could wax poetic about the approaching vertical summer.

Climbers are notoriously bullish about their preferences; even fellow climbers get sick of hearing the arguments over which form is best—sport climbing, trad climbing, bouldering, ice climbing, speed climbing, etc. An older, artificial outdoor wall in a remote corner of a small city, to that point, was certainly not the most sought-after climbing face, and I could imagine a group of hardcore, weathered climbers jibing at my choice. But I didn't care. I didn't care that the summer heat and humidity had already begun to hang heavy in the air, even at 9:00 in the morning. I didn't even care when the train dropped me off near the climbing wall and I found that there was, unfortunately, nobody else there aside from me, and no way of roping up. There was only the option of bouldering, climbing relatively low to the ground without a rope or harness. And then there was one minor detail: there were no soft floor mats, only hard wooden floor panels on which to fall. The Internet post had said nothing about bringing my own crash pad to cushion the tumbles, and in my overflowing eagerness to climb, I hadn't stopped to consider such an important aspect.

Nonetheless, undaunted and still enthusiastic, I hopped on the wall and tried a few sequences of hand and foot moves, then more difficult sequences to more precarious footholds, then turned a few sequences into full-fledged bouldering problems. I slipped and peeled off the wall a few times when the cruxes I had created were a little too ambitious for my own good, and took some shin-stinging falls onto the hardwood floor. By the time I was snacking on my little backpack lunch of cherries, a chocolate energy bar, and a cup of rice, my forearms were already pumped and swollen from the exercises. On one side of the climbing wall, a wide river meandered through the hills. The water was dotted with canoes lolling in the summer calm, and beyond the river, the foliaged hills ripened into mountains. It was difficult to judge the distance of the mountains from my valley seat beneath a line of trees, especially with mist rising from the banks of the river, but the peaks looked incredibly close—nearer to me because low-slung clouds encapsulated every terrestrial feature in a marvelous, hazy microcosm. There was an intermittent breeze which always seemed to inopportunely cease when I attempted another bouldering problem under the blistering sun on the baked resin handholds.

After a day of climbing, I was spent, but I was already dreaming of the multitude of climbs I'd attempt in the coming months. Many climbers tend to have an attention deficit when it comes to relishing the completion of the day—always looking to the next route, the higher grade, the following day's peak. I was no different.

On the train ride back to my apartment, I contemplated the peculiar interest in climbing that was now managing to lockjaw onto my day-to-day mindfulness. What was it about the methodical, vertical movement that made the act so irresistible to hordes of other mountain dirtbags? Or more precisely, why had I always felt most alive and stirred when I knew that a day of climbing lay ahead, and why did I always feel so fulfilled once that day was finished—even if that day turned out to entail bouldering on an old, vacant wall with stinging falls onto wooden paneling? Where, exactly, such a primal appreciation came from remained a badgering curiosity as the train wound through the green hills and I drifted to sleep in my corner of the train floor. (I hadn't had enough cash in my wallet to pay for an actual seat—a display of climbers' frugality at its finest). But prior to lulling off, I made a mental note to head outdoors for some real, non-artificial rock climbing as soon as I could. Smoothed, resin holds were fine, but I missed climbing on actual stone, and I longed for the dirt and grit that comes with it.

This also happened to be the unofficial starting weekend of the Korean monsoon season, and steady sheets of rain began to fall the following evening. The rainwater collected and pooled on the sidewalks outside my tiny apartment and rolled down the sides of the street in grimy, tube-like flows. It rained for days on end, the gray clouds in the sky bulbous and seemingly permanent. Other people in South Korea knew the frequent showers to be a regular part of summer, but the constant wetness drove an itchy climber like me to near-lunacy.

Left to my indoor devices, I donned my old habits—reading all the climbing literature that I could find, watching videos of inspiring, highly technical ascents and climbing competition highlights on the Internet, even downloading copious amounts of climbing podcasts to listen to while restlessly watching the downpour from my bedroom window, and all the while continuing to gnaw at the question: *just where does this affinity for climbing come from?*

The inglorious-yet-inspiring start of a climbing summer
Photo: Mike Reardon

2 | Climbing and human evolution

In the early 1970s, anthropologists and paleontologists were intrigued and somewhat flummoxed by a discovery in the ground in Egypt. Buried in the sand and dirt were fossil fragments of an extinct animal that would later be labeled *Parapithecus*. Scientists were able to deduce from the fragments (which amounted to mere bits of teeth, but nonetheless a valuable haul) that the animal was little—much smaller than a housecat, almost akin to a sewer rat in size. Additionally, they determined that *Parapithecus* lived 40 million years ago, swung from branch to branch in the treetops, and like many of the modern tree-dwellers, ate primarily leaves and berries.

But the certainties stopped there. The anthropological community was quickly divided on whether to classify *Parapithecus* as an early ape or an early monkey, given the lack of additional concrete evidence. On the one hand, detailed analysis of the teeth placed it more in line with the evolutionary dental path of apes—and thus, humans—while the tiny correlating body size of the animal put it closer to monkey status. As a reference, an adult male *Parapithecus* is believed to have weighed an average of 1.5 pounds, while the smallest modern great ape, the bonobo, weighs about 100 pounds at adulthood.

What was eventually decided, although the scientific community is still not in full agreement on this, was that *Parapithecus* is somewhat of a missing link between monkeys and apes, a possible common ancestor.

Whatever the case, it is certain that little *Parapithecus* was a climber, and that all *Homo sapiens*—from the infant crawling out of his crib to the dirtbag in a climbing harness rocking up Half Dome—are descended from it, or at least from some iteration of a fairly similar creature.

2. CLIMBING AND HUMAN EVOLUTION

Explaining how *Parapithecus* relates to modern rock climbing is somewhat like tracing how the very first paintbrush relates to da Vinci's *Mona Lisa*. But the great span of time pertaining to the relative correlation is eased by the fact that climbing has remained a pivotal part of evolution throughout evolution's lengthy course. It wasn't until very recently that climbing became so conspicuously absent from man's regular mechanical repertoire.

In the decades, centuries and millennia that would follow *Parapithecus's* existence, climbing trees would be all the rage in the animal kingdom, especially in the evolutionary boomtown that was *Parapithecus's* home: Africa. Thanks to a number of fossil discoveries over the years, paleontologists see Africa of 20 million years ago as a place teeming with monkeys and apes of all types and sizes.

To that point, during this era, the Early Miocene, some of the types of apes thrived, while many others fizzled into extinction. However, one of the species that would emerge successfully from the evolutionary melee would be *Sahelanthropus*, which is known to have existed around seven million years ago. Like *Parapithecus* is believed by many scientists to be a common predecessor of all primates, particularly monkeys and apes, *Sahelanthropus* is believed to be the keystone bridging two species of apes—humans and chimpanzees.

But if *Sahelanthropus* is a common ancestor for both us and chimpanzees, it has some explaining to do.

Stripping away humans' obvious civilized and cultural attributes like wearing clothes, riding vehicles, shacking up, and so forth, one of the most significant observable lifestyle differences between us and chimpanzees is that chimpanzees spend nearly half of their day, at least, climbing and lounging in the trees. Most humans (myself and my climbing-fanatical buddies excluded) spend most of their lives with both feet firmly on the ground.

So, how *Sahelanthropus* lived—whether it climbed like the chimpanzees or stayed on the ground like modern man—is particularly noteworthy.

It's also particularly unknown. There aren't many bones from which to deduce the nuanced locomotive points of

Sahelanthropus's day-to-day life, and certainly no complete bones directly related to climbing skills such as the metacarpals of the fingers or the radius and ulna of the arm.

So we are left to wonder if it was *Sahelanthropus* who chose being on the ground over climbing trees, or if it was one of *Sahelanthropus's* descendants. By the time the more well-known primates like *Neanderthals* were roaming the earth around 100,000 years ago, our evolutionary relatives were eschewing climbing for ground bipedalism. One of the landmark species in the history of man's climbing heritage is *Australopithecus afarensis*, which lived around 3 million years ago. Even that far back on mankind's evolutionary course, our primate relatives were spending a lot of time walking on the ground—upright and on two legs.

So what happened to all the climbing?

Dr. Peter Gray, an anthropology professor at the University of Nevada, Las Vegas, helped clarify some things for me one rainy afternoon, when the monsoon had forced me to remain indoors and in the books.

"Many scholars now believe that the evolution of human bipedalism occurred in two stages," Gray told me in an e-mail. "The first stage, around 6 million years ago, entailed the evolution of early hominins and subsequent australopithecine forms that still likely spent lots of times in trees; they had chimpanzee-sized bodies, but longer arms and longer finger and toe bones, the latter of which are interpreted as helping grab on to tree branches. The second stage, around 2 million years ago, entailed the evolution of committed bipedal forms. The interpretation is that these hominins no longer spent time in trees."

To the layman starting to feel overwhelmed with scientific minutiae, let's just say that the same anatomical characteristics that made our evolutionary ancestors good at climbing from tree to tree in the canopy also proved useful, millennia later, for ground activities such as grasping materials for making shelter, gathering food and other supplies and using tools. Like humans, chimpanzees grasp materials, gather supplies and use tools, and there is substantial shared DNA between humans and chimpanzees. In that case, is it safe to assume that some of the DNA that mankind shares with chimpanzees has to do with an affinity for climbing?

That's a complex question because it is nearly impossible to determine the degree to which climbing is a genetic adaptive response—like running as it relates to the fight-or-flight response—or a behavioral trait that is essentially learned. If one assumes climbing to be learned behavior, rather than genetically inherited, then science has proven that learned skills would not be passed straightforwardly from parent to offspring—a long-refuted concept called Lamarckism in evolutionary biology circles. So how do genetics play into all of it? A bird, as an analogy, is not born with the knowledge of how to fly, but genes obviously play a great role in shaping its ability to learn how to do so.

Some humans lack the behavioral fondness for climbing that chimpanzees seem to so readily possess. However, light the floor of a room on fire and any trapped human would undoubtedly exhibit an innate reaction to climb and clamor above the flames by whatever means—and scale up whatever structures—necessary to reach safety. Suffice to say, even if we have not been taught or conditioned to climb (that is, if we have not "learned" how to climb), there exists in all of us a general inborn knowledge of the necessary mechanics, although such knowledge might not exist to the degree that it does in chimpanzees.

It's reasonable to believe that we, modern humans, are capable of climbing far more than we do, and that our lack of a contemporary vertical life is owed as much to our conditioned habits and daily patterns as it is to any miniscule genetic dearth. It's important to mention that there are many hunter-gatherer communities around the world to this day that climb with great frequency—to gather primary dietary staples like honey, fruit and nuts, and to hunt tree-dwelling animals. Often, the children in these communities climb as well, and the youth play a vital role in assisting the adults in the gathering of food and the logistics of a given hunt.

Dr. Gray pointed this out as well, emphasizing that there are people who climb out of necessity rather than recreation. "There are various groups—the Aka people of the Congo, the Hadza people of Tanzania –in which men climb trees to get honey," Gray said. "I once watched in the Peruvian Amazon a guy ratchet up a palm to acquire fruits that were collected, bagged and sold; there are others who might climb precarious places to reach prized birds' nests. These variable types of climbing to obtain resources use a variety of techniques, some using more or less technology than others. They collectively remind us of ongoing abilities of humans to climb if circumstances warrant it."

Like chimpanzees, humans possess the multiple fingers and toes and long limbs primed for climbing. Over all the years of evolution, we have maintained much of the same physical characteristics that kept our ancestors in the trees millions of years ago. In one academic study from science departments at Dartmouth College, it was even determined that "derived aspects of the hominin ankle associated with bipedalism remain compatible with vertical climbing and arboreal resource acquisition"—in other words, our bipedal ankles are still fully capable of adept climbing.

"Watching kids climb is also interesting," Gray pointed out to me. "My daughters have long enjoyed playing on 'monkey bars'—which are really 'ape bars' given the shoulder mobility that we and other apes have but that monkey's don't—which could hint at our climbing past."

Many traits have evolved, but our physical tools for climbing remain largely unchanged. For me, this discovery, especially with the monsoon deluge going strong outside my deck window, merited further bookish investigation into the physicality of the climbing craft.

3 | The climber as vagabond

A climber is only as capable as the person on the other end of his rope, which makes finding a worthy climbing partner in a distant land somewhat of a cross between personality profiling and proctoring an exam of general climbing savoir-faire. Oddly, I moved to Asia, nearly 7,000 miles from my home in the United States, only to have my summer climbing partner be an old friend named Dan Kojetin, who happened to hail from the same sleepy Midwestern town as myself. Dan also happened to be cut from the same wanderlusting-turned-earth-wandering cloth that I was, and he had moved to South Korea seven years before I did. His intentions had been to attend graduate school in a foreign country and write a book chronicling South Korea's myriad of hiking trails.

I had barely corresponded with Dan at all since we were both in our early 20s, when we had both been counselors at the same summer camp in Minnesota. I recalled talking with Dan at a local bar when the camp was coming to its golden, seasonal close, after we had returned from guiding campers in sea kayaks through a maze of islands on Lake Superior. Dan mentioned then that the highlight of his trip had been paddling through sea caves at a place called Devil's Island, part of a chain known as the Apostle Islands, although he had gotten freaked out when a few young campers nearly got stuck in the narrowest cave openings. After regaling me with the tale, in the haze of beer and clunky rock music pouring through the bar's speakers, Dan said something to me about his objective to spend the next several years traveling the world and trad climbing. I didn't think too much of his aspirations at the time, figuring they were likely just late-night, alcohol-fueled ambitions and delusions, and we lost touch shortly after that summer.

In the ensuing years, I later learned, Dan actually kept good on his goals by climbing constantly and globetrotting from the United States to New Zealand, where he worked on a kiwi farm but had all of his climbing gear stolen. He soon bought new gear and headed to the climbing haven of Mount Arapiles in Australia, eventually winding his way back to the United States, to Yosemite in California. There, he slummed around the famous bouldering hub of Camp 4, sent a number of climbing routes in other states, scrounged up enough money to head overseas again, hit Nepal and base camped on Mount Everest—more of a travel destination for tourists than sport climbers, to the point where the very mention of Everest is often met with derision or vulgar bodily expressions of disapproval in climbing circles. But, as Dan told me, "If you're a climber and you're going to Nepal, you kind of have to see Everest."

As a caveat, he added, "When you get past Lukla, sure, just about everything is built for the tourists. But it's not gaudy, and it's understandable since there can't really be normal towns at such a high elevation. I did have a bad experience in Gokyo, though, where I had planned to stay for five days. I was kicked out of the guesthouse after just three days because a big tour group needed my room. I was bummed, so I just left Nepal altogether."

As much as he was a die-hard climber, Dan was an unabashed ski bum. He had devised a lifestyle that entailed traveling back to the United States from South Korea every winter, to work as part of the ski patrol at Powder Mountain in Utah—until the snow began to melt, at which point he'd fly back to Asia to teach a few English classes, chip away at his graduate school thesis, hike and climb.

The fact that Dan and I ended up living a few blocks from each other in South Korea was apropos; when I swung by his apartment to get up to speed on his international adventures and tell him that I was interested in doing a lot of climbing in the coming months, Dan said that his long-time climbing buddy had recently moved back to the United States. Such seeming abandonment had left Dan without anyone to climb with. So Dan, with his face tanned from a spring of hiking under the hot mountain sun day after day, couldn't help but smile at my craving for a summer of climbing. He was craving it too.

I quickly learned that Dan embodied a self-professed everyman-climber persona, not so much interested in ego-slinging and checking off all the highly technical routes in the guidebooks of the world. He was still a force to be reckoned with on the walls, certainly, and the previous year he had actually placed third in a regional South Korean sport climbing competition that saw the first and second place finishers earn trips to the country's national championships. It was a narrow miss of the big time, at least in regards to the competitive circuit. But Dan was drawn more to the relaxing afternoon pitches outdoors, a handful of challenging cruxes and, as he told me, topping it all off with some Korean barbecue and a beer or two.

Such insouciance suited my predilection just fine as well. I had vivid memories of taking mattresses off of bunk beds as a teenager, using them as bouldering crash pads, scrambling up slabs of dynamited rock cut on the sides of the highways while blaring music from the car speakers—my adolescence in all its rambunctious glory—to the chagrin of the traffic passing by. Clearly conventionality, in regards to climbing, had never concerned me much either.

A couple of hours passed while Dan and I reminisced over coffee in his apartment on a coincidentally sunny day, until he remembered some extra gear that had been taking up space on top of his closet. He opened a sliding ambry door to reveal a cardboard box full of quickdraws, ropes and loose carabiners. I was welcome to use any of it, he said, as it was largely gear that he'd collected over the years of having peripatetic climbing friends—ones who found it easier to give gear to Dan when they left Asia than to fly back to the United States loaded down with 25 extra pounds of climbing hardware.

Dan then suggested that we head out to a crag to try out some of the gear. I was itching to get back on a real rock, so we promptly filled a couple of water bottles, tossed the gear into a backpack and lit out for the nearest rock face. We zipped through traffic with a tumble of monsoon-season clouds looming overhead and a hilly line of trees on the horizon ahead of us. We cruised on back roads for a few miles and then parked on the embankment of a single-lane stretch of dusty concrete. We unloaded the car and hiked on foot through brush and broad-leafed greenery, along a path that wound and opened up to a clearing of tall rock faces. Under the creamy clouds, the gray rock cast a smattering of shadows on the ground—long and dark oblong forms that stretched the entire length of the clearing. In a series of a few steps, I saw a salamander wriggle into a fern patch and a line of crickets hop from the rocks into some tall grass. Then, looking up, I saw the shiny steel of new bolts in the rock faces. Despite the remoteness of our forest clearing, it was obvious that it was already a well-established haven for climbers in the area, and I asked Dan why he preferred to climb there.

"I like a lot of places," he said. "But the nice thing about these routes is that they were set by the local climbing club. Basically everyone in the club scattered around the rocks and got to develop his or her own climb." He unfolded his rope bag and added, "That type of thing would probably never happen back in the United States."

The South Korean Crag- developed by climbers, for climbers
Photo: Dan Kojetin

The clear advantage of having climbers of varying skill levels develop the crag was that the resulting routes were wildly diverse in difficulty, geometry and style. The route nearest to us, for instance, was rated a very undemanding 5.8 on the Yosemite Decimal System, which has been the standard rating measure for American climbers since the mid-20th Century. The route was an upward line with a few good handholds and steady, stable feet. But just a few feet away, on another section of the same rock, the route setter had chosen to bolt the perimeter of a more difficult, long and straight crack that called for repeated hand jams—squeezing your palm and fingers into the crack and torqueing them at the precise angle to create a firm, secure wedge. And just feet away from the hand jam route, behind the humps of a few enormous, free-standing boulders and regolith, was a cave that offered overhang movements and power routes rated up to 5.13 in difficulty. The bolts for the overhangs, however, looked expired and unsecure, which prompted Dan to share his personal climbing philosophy.

"It's all about risk management," he told me.

To his point, neither of us liked the idea of hanging on sketchy, bent bolts. "There are plenty of other routes around here," I said. "No need to take a chance on this one."

"My dad always tells me a story about World War I fighter pilots," Dan said. "Those guys were flying when aviation was still in its infancy and still really dangerous. Many pilots crashed their planes after flying just one or two missions. But there were some guys who survived dozens of missions, and when asked what their secret was to staying alive, do you know what they said?"

I shook my head and took a big gulp of cold water from one of our bottles.

"The pilots established a personal set of rules, entirely their own, but they stuck to those rules religiously," Dan said. "Most of the time if you break your own rules, you'll be fine; you'll get away with it. But you'll get in the habit of breaking your own rules, and that's when the really bad stuff happens."

"Definitely no climbing on the sketchy bolts today," I said.

"I'm also just an overly cautious person," Dan said, which was true, although the fact that he owned a motorcycle and enjoyed racing down powder hills on skis in the winter countered this notion somewhat. But he assured me with a smile that those were measured indulgences. "The more you do something, the more you learn it, and that lessens the risk. So do something a bunch, and do it well, and it won't be as dangerous."

We set up at the base of two stone spires that rose up perfectly parallel to one another. Dan took the lead and chimneyed up the rock using his legs and back to apply counter pressure against the parallel faces. I followed behind him, pausing to marvel at a pocket in one of the spires that housed the honeycombed remnants of a beehive, now thankfully abandoned. I felt sorry for the unlucky climber at some point before me who had likely reached into the pocket, enjoyed the momentary elation of finding a juggy handhold, only to be overcome an instant later by a raging swarm of irate, martyr-ready bees.

In a moment of repose, the beehive high up in the stone reminded me of what I had read about early primates gaining the ability to hold objects in their hands as a result of their climbing ability to grasp handholds in the trees. I shared the anecdote with Dan as we rested with our backs against the gray rock and ripped into a box of butter cookies.

"I guess we all were really born to climb," Dan said, and bit into two cookies dusted unintentionally with climbing chalk.

After we finished a handful of other climbs, we hiked back to our car, tossed our harnesses and backpacks in the trunk and drove home under the amber sun. Later that night, Dan, his girlfriend, and I lounged on the hardwood floor of his apartment and munched on a box of fried chicken ordered from a nearby restaurant. It was then that I learned of *Columbus*, a nearby climbing route that Dan had been working on for the past year.

"Everybody has their thing—their special climb," he explained. "I've never had a climb that I wanted to project. But this is one that has shut me down a few times. I know I can do it, so it has kind of turned into a project on its own."

"Tricky crux?" I asked.

"The crux is hard, but I can do it," he said. "It's more of an endurance issue—I need to improve my endurance, so we should climb a lot this summer."

We filled glasses with beer and looked at a few photographs that Dan had taken earlier in the day at the crag. I told Dan that I was ready and willing for as much climbing as his schedule would permit.

"The closest I've come to sending *Columbus* was falling on the last move," Dan said then, laughing at the memory of such a narrow miss.

"Heartbreaking," I said.

"Yeah, I guess, but not really," he said with typical dirtbag cheerfulness. "Sending it is not really a big deal to me. I don't want a single route to be the main goal. Let's just climb and not get caught up with projects."

4 | The physiology of climbing

One of the most bizarre climbing-related injuries I've ever heard of involved a man pulling a muscle in his neck as a result of days of belaying. I think all climbers can attest to the fact that the act of belaying—and tilting one's head up at an unnatural angle in order to maintain clear sight of your climbing partner on lead—isn't the most comfortable position, but this was the first incident I'd ever encountered in which the neck-craning actually proved hazardous.

More common climbing-related injuries include strained finger flexor tendons and annular ligaments, tendinitis in the elbows, torn rotator cuffs in the shoulders, tweaked knees and palm blisters galore, not to mention bone fractures, bulging discs in the spine and sprained ankles and wrists.

The point is that there are so many micro physiological processes involved in climbing that it would be nearly impossible to thoroughly explore the physicality of climbing in a single book—and even more daunting to do so in just one chapter. Considering the complex skeletal mechanics and communication with the nervous system, as well as genetic factors relative to climbing performance, there is as much nuance to climbing as any complex motor activity—certainly more than walking or running, and arguably more than swimming. Even discussion on a topic as seemingly basic as muscle memory, which is one of the most common concepts tossed around in climbing classes and technique drills, can get dizzyingly dense very quickly, as Francis Sanzaro, author of *The Boulder*, attests. "It is still up for scientific debate as to what muscle memory really is," Sanzaro says. "Some propose the capillary bed solution, or enzyme concentration, or DNA-containing nuclei, but regardless, it is much more complicated than simply building muscle for a move and feeling stronger two days later."

Sanzaro goes on to note that the concept of muscle memory likely involves repeated exercise as the body "learns to recruit more fibres," but even such an elementary description leaves the door open for numerous questions about muscles "learning," cell reproduction and neural efficiency, not to mention the open admission that science is still debating the concept of muscle memory itself, and that the exact physical demands of any two climbs might vary widely.

Fortunately, in order to explore how man's physicality developed to accommodate climbing, and how we still maintain and benefit from that climbing-centric anatomy today, one doesn't actually have to submerge himself under the elaborate and vast waters of climbing intricacies. This is because studies have shown that in physiological comparisons of traits such as hand strength, there's not that much difference between the best climbers of the world and non-climbers, and the differences only rear their heads when you start dividing the subjects into groups according to particulars such as body mass. As one study in the *British Journal of Sports Medicine* concluded: "Variance in climbing performance can be explained by a component consisting of trainable variables. More importantly, the findings do not support the belief that a climber must necessarily possess specific anthropometric characteristics to excel in sport rock climbing."

More to that point, although strength in relation to body mass tends to be significant in climbers, there isn't even a general consensus of one body type being more advantageous to climbing. Relatively tall climbers like my friend Dan note that their frame gives them a distinct reach advantage when lunging for far-away handholds or footholds. In fact, one's arm span in relation to height is actually called the ape index, a nod to our primate climbing heritage.

On the other hand, I have known shorter and stockier climbers who argue that they have better control of their center of gravity. A climber might have a lower ape index, or simply less linear reach with his arms, but also potentially less natural weight as a result, and such compact physical status could favor more power-oriented, dynamic movement on the wall.

So, body type deliberations in climbing circles are

potentially never-ending discussions. One of the smoothest climbers I have ever watched first-hand was Korean professional climber Jain Kim at a bouldering competition in Seoul. She cruised statically through insanely difficult bouldering problems that climbers of all sizes and body types struggled with repeatedly, and Kim is barely more than five feet tall.

Professional climber Jain Kim doing what she does best— making a complex route look easy during a competition
Photo: IFSC/OEWK/ Elias Holzknecht

As a result of the varied opinions on the best body type, the study of climbing's physicality really pans out to become a study of the anatomy possessed by each and every one of us, furthering the point that climbing isn't so much a niche recreation but an activity that we have all largely been designed to do from our inception, aside from learning the technical fine-tuning.

It's common for non-climbers to imagine climbers as muscular freaks of nature, as behemoths able to perform grotesque feats of strength like famed American rock climber John Bachar's legendary two-finger pull-ups. But anatomically, such preconceptions are misguided. The physical act of climbing actually stems from conscious movement of the bones, not conscious movement and operation of the neuro-muscular unit.

When I reached out to experts in the anatomy and kinesiology fields for comment on the muscular misconceptions, Dr. Phil Watts, an exercise physiologist at Northern Michigan University, told me, "In the early days, people expected rock climbers to have bodies similar to gorillas or weight lifters, but even a casual observation of the world's best climbers will reveal this to be untrue. What is important is climbing-specific strength relative to body weight. Since the maximum weight a climber has to work against is body weight, excessive muscle mass in the legs would be a detriment, adding weight without need for the added force."

It's prudent to look at which bone structures—more so than which muscular systems—have evolved in man to accommodate the climbing necessity; that is to say: *which bones developed as a result of man's affinity for climbing?*

The most blatant example of a bodily structure evolving to augment a climbing necessity isn't a bone in the arms or hands, as one might think. The humerus, radius, ulna, metacarpals and phalanges are all certainly vital components for climbing, but plenty of non-climbing animals such as dogs or deer have arms (rather, forelimbs) and appendages—hoofed, clawed or otherwise—that are analogous in some ways to the hands of man but lacking the prehensile capability.

In fact, the bone that perhaps most obviously indicates that man was a climber and is still fully capable of a sustained climbing lifestyle is the collarbone. Specifically, the angle at which the collarbone has evolved, aiding in holding man's forelimbs at his side rather than in front of his body—where they exist for dogs, deer and the like—indicates that man's arms were meant to aid in much more complex and multi-dimensional movement than the forelimbs of the quadrupeds.

A dog, for example, can run only forward, and can do so only on the ground due to the skeletal structural limitations and placement of its forelimbs; that same dog would be relatively incapable of moving abruptly vertically without also moving forward. All dogs can climb stairs, but scaling a ladder is virtually impossible for even the most dexterous breeds. Even if a precocious dog could somehow get up a ladder, the dog would never be able to operate its forelimbs independently the way that primates can given the primates' collarbone and lateral positioning of the pectoral girdle.

There are other anatomical structures worth noting in relation to climbing as well. Take, for example, the human brain. Scientists have a host of theories as to why man is so much more intelligent than any other creature on the planet. The genetic gap between man and chimpanzee is rather small, but within that smidgen of DNA difference resides mankind's ability to create both written and spoken complex languages, build complex mechanical structures such as computers and cell phones, develop and enforce legal systems, ponder the universe and reflect on his own mortality. Nobody knows exactly how—or more aptly, exactly why—our brains developed with the great capabilities that they retain. However, I've found that in all the theories about the evolution of man's brain, the physicality of climbing and the grand role it played in the process seems to get woefully overlooked.

Let's return to using a dog for comparison, in order to illustrate the importance that the physiology of climbing has played in man's development to present-day thinker, stockbroker, doctor, train conductor or college co-ed.

At some point in man's extensive pedigree—long before we were "man" at all, and before the primate mammalian iteration of our existence—we could have been like the dog—quadrupeds with forelimbs in front of us in the manner of most other large terrestrial vertebrates.

But in evolving to accommodate vertical movement, and thus shaping our anatomy more closely to its present day architecture, it is possible that mankind gained the ability to be a much more sensory-diverse species. Climbing, and particularly the anatomical changes brought about because of it, allowed man not only an additional plane of existence on which to explore, but also supplementary biological advantages as a result of having arms at his sides capable of autonomous movement. With lateral limbs and hands free to reach and grab at nearly all angles, the mouth was no longer needed as a grabbing biological feature. Quite frankly, man was finally free to hold his head high, look around and take in the natural world with a new degree of sensory awareness. Objects could be examined, held, smelled, sniffed and licked, which some experts have argued necessitated growth of the head—and certainly expansion of the mind—which, in turn, influenced the shape and development of man's brain.

Climbing became so essential to the physiology of our primate forefathers that the present-day human body devotes a substantial degree of its anatomical design to the versatile command and control of the arms. It's easy to consider our upper limbs as mere accessories to our more important thorax, which houses the vital organs. In fact, an examination of the muscular-skeletal composition of the upper torso clarifies things. Many of the hefty bones of the thorax, such as the breastplate and the ribs, play a role in encasing or bulwarking the heart and lungs.

The muscles of the thorax, on the other hand, tell a different story.

I had already looked into the placement of the collarbone. But when it came to the muscles, I sought out Mabel Elsworth Todd's classic book on human movement, *The Thinking Body*, and learned that a vast majority of those muscles in the thorax play a small role in encasing and safeguarding the heart and lungs—after all, bone serves as a much tougher material for shielding and protecting vital organs than muscle anyway—and a large, direct role in arm dynamism. Choose a random bone located in the midsection of any human, and trace the muscles that are attached to that bone. There's a good chance that the other end of that muscle plays a role—either partially or substantially—in the movement of the shoulder. The extensive network of shoulder muscles connects to nearly all the major bones of the upper torso, which is precisely why the shoulders and arms can move so powerfully.

One can only read so much about muscle power and the physicality of climbing before a craving to actually climb becomes too intense to ignore, too sizeable to keep at bay with academic literature and glossy crag photographs. As I read Todd's comments, I found myself crimping the edge of my desk, and imagining that my empty coffee mug was a hollowed pocket deep enough for fingers to fit comfortably inside. I was also prone to reaching over my bookshelf from time to time in pure fantasy of lunging for an imaginary handhold—the muscles of my entire upper body honed in on sticking the landing and maintaining the grip over the dusty line of books in my apartment. Clearly this was a unique form of cabin fever at its strongest, and it was time to get out and go climbing.

5 | All in the groove

The wall, at first clearly vertical but viciously curved and concave farther up, hadn't looked so diverse from the ground. Having managed to clip my rope past the first five bolts on a clear-skied Korean morning, I chose to avoid climbing over a steep rim, instead opting for a route that I thought would be fairly pedestrian. Dan had me on belay, and when I tilted my head out of the wall's concave pocket and looked down, I could see him staring up at me in his dark-rimmed glasses and shouting words of encouragement. My left hand was gripping a small nugget hold near my torso, and my right arm was fully extended to a hold that had a positive edge but was slanted at a challenging, wrist-twisting angle. I was, for the time being, stuck. Any substantial movement to my left or right would amount to a change in the location of my center of gravity over my feet—also edged on minuscule nubs.

At one point, I purposely let go of the right-handhold with the intention of reaching for another quickdraw on my harness. I methodically began to unclip the quickdraw from its harness loop, but it was useless. Even such subtle movement involved rotating my shoulder slightly, and I could sense that such movement would set off a chain reaction of unwanted and uninviting body mechanics: My shoulder rotation would cause my torso to turn, which would pull my hips away from the wall, which would peel my hands from their precarious handholds, and gravity would top off the spectacle. I would be ripped from the wall's face and dangling in the air, on the rope, in mere fractions of a second.

"Take your time," Dan shouted to me from the ground. He squinted and changed his belay position to get a better assessment of my stymied progress.

Dan was right: Going slow was the best solution, as sudden movements would only create more momentum, more force pulling me off the wall. Yet, time was also a negative factor. The longer I stayed in the concave spot with my arms outstretched and my legs flexing on tiny footholds, the more I could feel my strength starting to diminish at a seemingly exponential pace. I was trying my best not to let the extraordinary and supreme climbing apprehension, that I would fall, enter my mind.

In an essay titled "Roping Up," David Roberts writes, "The rope to which I had tied myself dragged me into commitment. As we pushed upward on the scary, hollow-ringing flakes of rock, the rope allowed our trespass: Without it, there would have been no such tiptoeing in the sky. As the climb got hard, and the hours of concentration devolved into trance, we became the most privileged of explorers, for there is no terrain so exquisite and unknowable as vertical rock. And when everything, even lift itself, hung in the balance, the rope held us together."

It's such reliance on not only rope, but one's own physical movement and the wall face itself, that makes climbing a captivating merger of man's physical abilities and fears—and the natural world that envelopes those elements.

"You've got another bolt above your head, within an arm's reach," Dan shouted.

I gradually looked up and saw the silver bolt glistening like a blade's edge. I decided to try again to release the quickdraw from my harness loop. My left hand, white-knuckled from crimping the little nugget, was starting to burn from the tensed muscles. I tried to relax my hand, to lean back on the hold as much as my wedged position would allow, but my attempt didn't provide much space or relief.

I took a few slow breaths. The temperature was hot, especially against the searing rock face. I could feel sweat between my fingertips and on my palms.

"You are not at the summit and yet you feel so alive," writes Eric Swan in a piece titled "Zen and the Art of Climbing." "With a heightened sense of focus, you lock in on the next hold and continue your climb." The quotation ultimately asserts climbing to be a matter of delicate movements and small spaces as much as epic ascents, great distances and grand altitudes.

But at that moment, I felt that I couldn't continue my climb. The quickdraw carabiner had rotated on my harness loop, which required more subtle movement to unclip it and raise it with my right hand. All of this was serving to make me think even more about my increasing weakness on the wall.

"If you have to reflect on your internal states during a climb, it is often the sign of impending disaster," says author Stephen M. Downes in a climbing piece titled, "Are You Experienced." Downes asserts, "The process of self-reflection can sometimes be helpful but often involves accessing just the wrong kinds of internal states, beliefs about the route, your abilities, the potential fall, and so on." He suggests breathing slowly and focusing on calming your nerves and slowing your heart rate—matters with tangible, controllable results—rather than honing in on the more weighty, reflective matter.

I tried to distance myself from any thoughts about my own abilities and simply accepted a truth that I was capable of doing the moves. Perhaps I wouldn't be graceful, and I certainly wouldn't coast up the wall with style. But I was at least capable of the geometry—capable of getting from my current point A to the successive, nearby point B, and so on.

Finally, I got the quickdraw unclipped, outstretched my arm, stood up on my legs, and then felt the quickdraw carabiner hook into the bolt with a loud click. "Zen and the Art of Climbing" also notes, "In climbing the answers are always right in front of you; insights and progress come from 'seeing things as they are.'"

I took more slow breaths and raised the rope to the quickdraw. I tensed my left hand tightly against its nugget hold, pressed my feet into their holds, and at last clipped the rope into the bolted quickdraw.

Suddenly, as if breaking free of some psychological membrane, I was able to act and move comfortably. I continued my slow movement up the gray face, turning my hips and finding footholds first, then moving on them and finding positive holds for my hands. I didn't fall—at least not on that particular sequence in the wall's concave pocket—and I felt wonder at such an abrupt shift from being hindered completely to finding motion once again.

When Dan and I were together again on the ground, I explained the situation to him. He hadn't been able to fully see my predicament in the glare.

"I felt helpless up there," I told Dan. "It was like every move just led to more instability."

"There's always a way," Dan said, ever so Zen-like. "Or, at least you have to tell yourself that there always is."

We packed up our gear and wandered into a restaurant for cold beer. The cozy back room was packed with people watching an international soccer game on a large TV. When the Korean team scored a goal, the room erupted with shouts and cheers, everyone ecstatic and brimming with pride for their country's team.

Dan and I watched the last few moments of the game, but my mind was still on the earlier climbing route. I had, for a long time, known climbing to be an odd and fascinating unity of composure and potential chaos. But the summer's early immersion was quickly giving me new perspectives on how the physical hyperreactive aspects were inseparable, perhaps even secondary, to a deeper subliminal groove.

Gary Pisano on the classic "Groover", a 1,000 foot water groove on eastern America's tallest and most revered rock, Laurel Knob, NC
Photo: Mike Reardon

6 | The mental game of climbing

I once read a profile of Yvon Chouinard that appeared in *The New Yorker* in the 1970s. Chouinard would eventually go on to found the outdoor-clothing juggernaut Patagonia and work on a number of worthy environmental conservation causes. But at the time *The New Yorker* article was written, Patagonia, as a clothing company, was in its infancy. It wasn't even called Patagonia yet, rather, Chouinard Equipment, in reference to the climbing hardware that Chouinard handmade before he ever started manufacturing clothing.

Chouinard spent much of his early adulthood living as a drifter, wandering frugally to various climbing crags across the United States. He also served in the military, during which time he was stationed in South Korea. He spent much of his free time in South Korea climbing the mountains around Seoul, and much of the country's current climbing culture owes a debt of gratitude to Chouinard's routes and impact.

What I remember most from the magazine article was Chouinard's personal recounting of an accident he had while climbing the north face of Crooked Thumb, a shoulder of Teewinot Mountain in Wyoming's Grand Teton National Park. The incident provides a model of the petrifying effect—the psychological vice grip—that the mental aspect of the sport can have on anyone, even an expert climber like Chouinard.

Chouinard, as the article explained, had climbed high and reached an overhanging section of Crooked Thumb. With a swami belt of tubular webbing looped around his waist in the protection style of the era, he attempted to climb up and over the jutting rock feature. Cascade Canyon loomed far below. He made it close to the edge of the overhang before his arms pumped out and a loose handhold broke from the rock face. Chouinard went into a dangerous fall—more than 150 feet—until he snapped to a halt at the end of his rope. He sustained some bruises and a deep leg laceration, but still managed to create enough momentum from his hanging point in midair to swing to some decent handholds. His partner rappelled down to him and together they traversed a ledge and eventually descended the mountain.

The experience had a profound effect on Chouinard— not because of the wounds, which healed in time. Rather, it was his psychological assessment of his own abilities, and the miscalculation about the sequence of moves, that proved more damaging than any physical injuries. He spent several of the following years trying to regain his mental composure. When he'd find himself in comparable climbing scenarios, his limbs would shudder. The physical mechanics of climbing, which had once been second nature to him, were extraordinarily tough as a result of his mental hang-ups.

The mind, as related to an active endeavor like climbing, can be an overwhelming subject, as it's much easier to measure physical performance than to quantify something more abstract like mental focus in the heat of the activity. Still, I couldn't help but wonder about the possible converse to Chouinard's anecdote: if the sport had the power to spoil one's mental precision altogether for years, as it had done for Chouinard, it seemed logical that the craft of climbing could also create a reverse effect and lead a person to profound mental clarity.

To get some insight on this, and to approach the concept from an authoritative angle, I reached out to Dr. Rebecca Williams, a climber and clinical psychologist who combined her passions for scaling rock walls and studying mental health into a successful business endeavor called Smart Climbing. The idea behind Williams' Wales-based brand, of which she serves as the director, was initially to improve people's climbing through a number of workshops focused on the mental components of climbing—lessening anxiety, visualization, mindfulness. As a result, Williams has become a leading figure in the growing and ever-evolving field of climbing psychology.

Yvon Chouinard assessing his gear during one of his many climbing trips in the 1960s
Photo: Glen Denny

"There is still a bit of a mentality that one just needs to get physically stronger to improve his or her climbing, and most of the information out there is based on top climbers and what worked for them—very individually specific and, at times, not based on a thorough self-reflection—rather than science," Williams said of the idea of studying the mind in a field that is so blatantly focused on the physical. "There actually isn't as yet a whole lot of science from climbing on which to base training decisions. It's mostly coming from related disciplines and then being adapted to climbing. That should change over time."

Williams acknowledged the critics who think the study of climbing's cerebral side is useless. Even in hyperbole, saying that climbing is more of a mental game than a physical one, which Williams has noted in the past, is bound to ruffle some feathers.

"When I have written articles for magazines, I usually get a mixed response," she explained to me. "For example, I wrote one post about the importance of setting process goals rather than outcome-based goals based in research, and I had about 75 percent of people saying how useful it was and 25 percent saying, 'What a load of rubbish.'"

But as climbing has grown in popularity, so too have all angles of its scholarship. Many people have come to see climbing as a multifaceted and unique endeavor—what Williams refers to as a "slow acceptance" of the craft's mental game—which means seeing climbing as a sport worthy of study beyond the physical gripping and grunting that it takes to muscle up a wall.

"Climbing is pretty unusual in sports psychology terms, as I work with climbers who don't have coaches and who are not competing," she said. "In many other sports, one is generally working alongside a team of people with those who are competing."

And in what other ways is it unusual?

"The unique elements come from the height—an objective danger which we seem evolutionarily programmed not to like, despite our simian ancestry—and the fact that patterns of movement are continually altering," Williams said. "Yes, there are 'standard' movements such as a heel hook or crimping, but the combinations of moves are unique to each route, and it's difficult to drill them as you would, say, a gymnastics routine or a tennis swing. Climbing really is vertical chess. I've often thought it would be fascinating to do neuropsychological profiles of the best climbers because their visuospatial ability must be very highly developed with the way they 'read' routes so quickly; I bet it would show up on tests."

At this point, I wondered how Williams initially found her way to researching the psychological underpinnings of climbing, since the subject wasn't exactly the lightest topic to mull over on lazy afternoons at a crag. But it turned out that Williams had gravitated to it initially not for the purpose of helping others, but the purpose of helping herself.

"I started doing gymnastics at four years old, and I competed a lot," she said. "I was always quite a tomboy, but I was also a perfectionist and I had a big capacity for training. I was good at following programs and continuing when things got tough."

However, Williams' gymnastics ambitions got derailed when she was still quite young after a severe asthma attack and subsequent hospitalization, which resulted in crippling anxiety and a loss of self-confidence regarding her abilities to physically meet the demands of that sport.

"When I eventually discovered climbing, in my late 20s, it was quite by accident, but I was instantly hooked," she said. "I loved the combination of thinking moves through, moving my body precisely, and I had that instant hit of wanting to get better at it. It was only after a couple of years when I had learned the skills well enough to not have to think everything through each time on lead that suddenly my old fears from gymnastics came back to bite me. It took quite a while to figure out what to do about it, and at the time there was no sports psychology stuff on climbing at all. It was a case of applying clinical psychology models of anxiety and being systematic about exposure work, as well as understanding where the anxiety came from, which helped me."

I immediately noticed a common thread in Williams and Chouinard's accounts, which was anxiety and apprehension manifesting to inactivity or aggravation. Or, to put it in the more common climber's vernacular: being scared shitless. There's an academic concept known as negativity bias, in which uncomfortable and unpleasant experiences play on one's psyche more so than comfortable and positive events. The idea pertains to practically all aspects of learning and evolution, but apply the concept specifically to climbing and it is understandable how a single, harrowing moment on a wall can be psychologically enduring—even if there are countless positive and non-detrimental moments to offset it.

I told Williams about Chouinard's account of taking years to work up the courage and ability to climb at the levels he had achieved prior to his big fall. Williams said, "It's interesting because most of the clients I work with have not actually had a bad fall or even seen a bad fall, so they are anxious in anticipation of something happening, without real evidence for it."

In other words, I knew that unease could hit climbers from all figurative angles: anxious if they have fallen, and anxious even if they haven't fallen.

"The best approach with anticipatory anxiety is to systematically test out the fears—an example would be falling practice to help learn how to fall well," Williams explained. "However, such practice often only goes so far, in my view, as the real fear can be being out of control. And when you are falling, you are out of control. So I have found that mindfulness practice is often a good approach used in combination with the behavioral experiments to find out what happens when you do fall. Mindfulness is used to help detach oneself from one's thoughts and learn that, no matter how real they seem, they are only thoughts, and to direct thoughts more to useful things—such as how best to climb a route rather than ruminating about a possible fall which hasn't yet happened."

Chouinard's systematic and calculated—albeit, ultimately unsuccessful—attempt to climb the overhanging wall spoke to another point that Williams made: climbers aren't typically the reckless adrenaline junkies that their penchant for dangerous heights might suggest, which harkens back to her chess analogy.

"What has been fairly soundly disproven is the idea that climbers are thrill seekers—for the most part they are not," Williams said. "Climbers like novelty but not risk for risk's sake. Previous research tended to lump climbers in with base jumpers and free fallers, when the mindset is quite different."

So if the mental pursuit of the vertical isn't necessarily only about the thrill, what drives many climbers?

Williams said, "I think perhaps there is some commonality amongst climbers about overcoming things they find challenging or even scary, and the latest research suggests that climbers are weak at emotional expression—and possibly personal relationships—and they find that climbing provides a way of maintaining self-esteem and emotional regulation. Certainly many climbers I have worked with have a deep need to prove themselves as worthwhile somehow, but it's something I have refrained from saying, as I feel it's the elephant in the room and perhaps people may be too fragile to have it said out loud."

That need to prove one's worth can be especially challenging when it comes to training though, as climbing can be largely communal in practice. "You have to not mind other people witnessing your 'failures,'" Williams said. "Climbing is such a small community, and many climbers feel that 'everyone' is judging their performance. So being able to blank out social comparison is a good skill. Most adults will opt for saving face rather than being seen to fail. All this becomes especially true once you need to break through the inevitable plateau that any climber faces, where it is about working very hard on weaknesses and paying attention to details to make small gains in performance."

I considered what she said about plateauing, and I imagined the mental clarity that could result from climbing as a gleaming prize sitting atop an insanely tough route. But I immediately realized the error in my thinking—the notion of clarity existing as an end target was faulty. Clarity was, in actuality, something to be obtained in constant progression.

"The brain has a kind of cutoff point to prevent injury, and many people's idea of their maximum effort is not actually their maximum effort," Williams said. "I tend to get clients to work on this by using a stopwatch and having them hang on some holds for as long as possible, and it turns out that when they think they are about to fall off, they can usually hang on for another 40 seconds or longer. There is a similar psychological barrier that prevents people from trying things that they think are 'impossible.' For example, an F6c [5.11b] climber thinks he can't climb F7a [5.12a], but he has never actually attempted it. So another exercise I might do would be to ask him, 'How do you know?' and then get him to try the F7a [5.12a] route. Usually he'll get farther than he thought, and so it opens up a possibility in his mind that it's possible, which suddenly frees him up to climb harder."

Williams referred to the idea of complete mental clarity while climbing as part of a flow experience, which sounded about as Zen as any concept could be without actually referencing Buddhist texts. "When you have a flow experience or peak experience, which are documented psychological phenomena, your sense of time gets disrupted, you experience a kind of moment of perfection, and in that moment you can feel connected to something bigger than yourself," she said. "It's that absorption in the mental and physical challenge which creates the flow experience, and it can leave you with a profound sense of peace or even a high which connects with the spiritual."

It all sounded a bit mystical. However, there was hard science at the root of the flow experience that Williams referenced, in the form of natural synchronization of dopamine, norepinephrine, serotonin, anandamide and endorphin production that occurs in the neurology of one's brain. More specifically, all of those—essentially the body's main pleasure-inducing chemicals—being produced at optimal levels results in mental acuity and responsive physical performance. Of the more than a dozen categorical factors that spur such a chemical onslaught and subsequent harmonizing to prompt the flow experience, one is the realization of the risks and consequences of a given activity—in the case of climbing, falling and injury.

I hadn't initially set out to discover any flow experience in my summer of climbing obsession, nor was I clear on exactly how to obtain such mental and physical singularity. In fact, the more I thought about it in the following days, the more it seemed like something that couldn't be actively sought. Yet, I couldn't help but long for such lucidity in the simple act of climbing, a clarity that surpassed climbing's psychological or physical roots. The flow experience was out there, somewhere in the vertical, and the way to find it was to simply let it be.

Professional climber Juliane Wurm figuring out the move sequence during a bouldering competition— vertical chess, in a fundamental sense
Photo: IFSC/OEWK/ Elias Holzknecht

7 Motivations on the mountains

Seoul in the summer could be particularly congested in the morning: dense lines of traffic in great concrete reticulations, the streets sunbaked, and the glassy skyscrapers edge-to-edge and gleaming above whole the rush hour mess. But if one was able to break free from the urban crunch, the city stretched out its legs in the form of pastoral roads paved over green hills and flanking rice patties to the southeast. Low-slung clouds with occasional precipitation kept the outlying forests wet and beautifully glossy—dense walls of shining green leaves and vines of all tones—along with roadside shops selling fresh seafood or hand-held fans to beat the heat.

It was on one of these misty mornings that I hitched a ride to a crag at a mountain known as *Namhan-san*—translated as *The Mountain to the South of the Han River*—with a local climbing group from the Astroman Climbing Gym in Seoul. I sat in the backseat of an old jeep, squeezed in between hiking packs and rope bags, and watched the sprawl of the city dissipate and ease into the idyllic outskirts. The low-pressure system ascended and broke apart in a matter of hours, revealing blue sky without a single cloud.

Our climbing outfit was small—six people in total cramped in the jeep, most of them middle-aged and friends of the group's leader, Stanley Hong. Nearly 50 years old, Stanley was a graceful and compact climber who hadn't even started climbing until he was in his mid-40s. I had met Stanley often for midday beers and climbing conversation long before the start of my summer, and it was a pleasure to be finally climbing with him outdoors.

We parked the jeep, distributed the hardware, and began the approach to the bosky crag. We hiked up a steep grassy hill adorned with ancient Korean graves. Large burial mounds of smoothed dirt marked with hand-carved wooden signs looked as if they had swelled up from deep within the earth, when in fact, the mounds had been tenderly and lovingly crafted by the families of the dead. The earthen mounds encased the buried bones of elders from the region, and hiking past them on the way to a handful of climbing routes, on a sparkling morning, was enough to remind me of the grand karmic algebra—pursuit of pleasure, action and reaction in one endless loop, until the loop actually does finally and eternally end and you're left to be someone else's crag-side hump of dirt, mere compost for those dense walls of shiny green leaves. In other words, enjoy the climbing—and life, in general—while you can.

Once we reached the crag, we harnessed up and spent the morning on a number of routes, mostly single-pitch lines with a couple of shoulder-pumping overhang cruxes that hovered around 5.10-level and boasted Korean names that translated to *Love Mountain* and *Success*, among other fitting epithets. A pause for a lunch of instant noodles cooked over a camping stove gave me a free minute to walk around the crag and explore the rock faces-less-climbed. There were other groups of climbers working their way up routes as well during lunchtime, but beyond them, the steep face of rock ceased and the ground rose in a gentler incline, more manageable for scrambling up by foot.

Hiking to a higher elevation got me thinking about the kindred connection of the two—hiking and sport-climbing. They exist now on different planes of the recreational spectrum, but if they share any derivation, it lies in the pastime propensities of the previous centuries. I found this out after returning from *Namhan-san* and immersing myself in books and articles on world cultures of yesteryear—books with stirring titles like *Unfinished Revolutions* and *The European Witch-craze of the Sixteenth and Seventeenth Centuries and Other Essays.*

The books on culture were necessary, as the question *Why did people climb in the several centuries preceding our own?* was really an examination of larger issues taking root in the various societies at the time. Apes and earliest man climbed for food and survival, but what spawned the mountaineering boom that eventually led to making a sport out of its most difficult and athletic mechanics?

As much as one can passably condense hundreds of years of cultural history into a few stacks of library books and bookmarked websites, and then condense those gems into a few scribbled notebook pages while resting from a sunny day of climbing near a Buddhist gravesite, allow me to inform the reader here that the answer is: it's complicated.

That's not to say that it is unknowable, however. If the climbing culture nowadays owes a nod to slick marketing and the allure of being part of a subculture, then climbing culture in the past tipped its cap to necessity and an alignment with the burgeoning mainstream cultures of the period. But one must look farther back than the 19th Century to view sport climbing's embryonic stages in the form of alpinism. For example, legend has it that in my neck of the woods, Asia, around 200 B.C., a Chinese ruler, Shih Huang Ti, sent out a band of explorers to climb several of the tallest mountains in Asia. Supposedly this far-reaching early expedition even reached parts of present-day South Korea. And why were these explorers climbing? They scaled the peaks because ruler Shih had instructed them to seek out and find "the elixir of life"—essentially a fountain of youth.

Needless to say, motivations for mountaineering evolved in the ensuing eras. Survey the history of the 17th, 18th and 19th centuries (although you could probably skip the book about witch-crazes) and you'll find that it was notions of conquest and subjugation—not necessarily hankerings for undiscovered magic elixirs—that permeated nearly every aspect of life. In fact, alpinism and mountaineering were born partially out of a rather disproportional preoccupation with conquest around the world at the time. Anything could be conquered, and as an example, consider the degree to which countries built up their armies in preparation for acquiring other lands and people: There were nearly one million serving soldiers in Central and Western Europe in the early 1700s, compared to just 300,000 serving soldiers 100 years before that. And naturally, the countries had to do something with such massive armies, so all of this huffing and puffing amounted to staggering amounts of war—several dozen wars in France, England and Spain in a 220-year span, from 1480 to 1700.

Conquest wasn't just the popular military ethos of the time. In one of the more titillating sections of the otherwise straight-laced book, *Early Modern Europe*, I read about the church framing sex in a subjugating manner, with the Catholic policy of the time contending that a man should always position himself on top during intercourse.

So the idea of "conquering" a mountain back then, staking one's proverbial flag atop nature's most intimidating structure, fit well within the disposition of the era. However, it was the widespread emergence of a leisure class that also gave mountain climbing credence and allowed the idea to mature into a full-on activity independent from any larger incentives.

Ed Feuz leading and Dr. Thorington climbing, ice fall of Freshfield Glacier on way to Mt Barnard, 1922

Photo in public domain courtesy of The Henry S. Hall Jr. American Alpine Club Library

As I found while perusing numerous books on how old-time Europeans spent their day-to-day, it turned out that when the people of Europe—the people who controlled much of the world at the time—were not busy saluting in their respective armies, they had an increasing amount of free time on their hands. This was due to a number of factors, most notably the rise of widespread industrialization and wealth that allowed for leisure pursuits. Such free time usually amounted to raucous card games and book reading, maybe some cotillion or an inordinate amount of church socializing. I could only read about so many Victorian board games in a single sitting, but I assure you that those were present in the period as well.

All of these leisure activities might have stayed indoors, and likely would not have extended to the rugged mountains, had it not been for another keystone—a sudden and pressing widespread interest in science and nature. Steadily, organizations aimed at studying nature began to pop up all over Europe—in Paris, London and elsewhere. These organizations began utilizing new mechanical technology for analyzing the natural world, and even more significantly, they began to display specimens of the natural world in the museum exhibit format that we are familiar with today—often referred to as "chambers of wonders" or "cabinets of curiosities" at the time. These early museum showcases displayed rare flora specimens and taxidermied fauna, as well as rocks such as fossils and geodes.

The fact that the countries showcased their geodes should not go overlooked. Geology was all the rage 200 years ago, and more specialized subfields like paleontology were attempting to explain our past by digging into the dirt. This coincided with the publication of remarkable natural history books like Charles Darwin's *On the Origin of Species* and the anonymously authored *Vestiges of the Natural History of Creation*. One statistic I read noted that the European middle class in the mid-1800s bought five times as many geology books as fiction novels—a big shock considering this was also the age of literary giants like Charles Dickens and Jane Austen.

7. MOTIVATIONS ON THE MOUNTAINS

Mountaineering turned out to be the perfect confection to result from this strange brew of conquest and dominance mentality, leisure recreation and a substantial interest in rocks. And the first real mountaineering icon to be born as a result of it was Alfred Wills, who climbed the Wetterhorn in the Alps in September of 1854.

Wills lived what can only be described as a veritable double-life, which was common for the Victorian-era mountaineers. Born and educated in London, he was a whiz kid who dominated multiple academic fields, passed the Bar, became a noted judge, and by all accounts threw himself into his work with the utmost fervor and professionalism and was knighted later in life. But aside from such refined academic and career ascendancy, Wills had a hankering for roughing it—to the extent that he actually spent part of his honeymoon on a glacier in the Alps.

Wills hadn't been climbing for very long when he ascended the Wetterhorn, and it wasn't even the first time the mountain had been climbed. But what made Wills' Wetterhorn ascent remarkable was that he deliberately eschewed any scientific purpose for his climb, which broke from the academic norms of previous mountaineers, as well as his own background as an esteemed scholar, but ultimately lightened the amount of hardware he would have to schlep up the mountainside. Instead, Wills' climb was driven by competition. He made a wager with a couple of hunters from Chamonix, France, that he could beat them to the summit. The race to climb the Wetterhorn ended eventually with the hunters and Wills finishing together and disregarding the competitive aspect of things. Nonetheless, leisure climbing with a degree of sport, rivalry and competition was born.

Soon the notion of alpine clubs was en vogue—which essentially made Victorian-era climbing a team sport, rather than an individual pursuit. And it wasn't just a man's game, although men got a majority of the publicity. An English climber named Lucy Walker waded through the sexism of the era and made a name for herself in the 1860s and 1870s by making countless ascents, including the first female ascent of the Matterhorn. And in the United States, although climbing didn't yet have the public seal of approval like it did in Europe, Julia Archibald Holmes climbed to the top of Pikes Peak in the Rocky Mountains in 1858.

A few years later, an amateur botanist from Austria named Conrad Kain immigrated to Canada, claimed a number of ascents in the Canadian Rockies, and in the process shaped mountain climbing into a North American pastime largely cast in the European mold. Mountaineering in North America was further solidified with the formation of the American Alpine Club in 1902 and the Alpine Club of Canada in 1906.

In a matter of years, it seemed that climbing was everywhere, and a new age of mountaineering was upon the entire world. It's impossible to know how or when climbing might have evolved if it hadn't been for Europe's historical cultural and intellectual course, how an inherent desire to scale the vertical fragments of the world as well as the horizontal land and sea would have manifested itself in ages of increasing industrialization, technology and general world-wonderment. By the time Sir Edmund Hillary famously ascended to the top of Mount Everest on May 29, 1953, mountaineering was a firmly established pastime, but the successful summit owed everything to the practices of people all over the globe who had come before it.

In the end, when I shelved the last batch of books and trudged back home in the Korean heat, my remaining curiosities could be answered with the cleanest line: Man of the previous centuries climbed simply because the rocks and mountains were there. Whatever greater cultural tastes might have existed to get men and women outside and to the base of the mountains, it was an initial cognizance of the peaks and crags that stirred in so many people a desire to apply other justifications to the splendid pursuit.

I did some easy bouldering that night and thought about the Buddhist mounds at *Namhan-san*, the bones of the long-dead buried near the crag and immortalized with carved wood. I thought also about how Alfred Wills is now immortalized on his own famous Wetterhorn route—an arête there is named in his honor. In a moment of rest, I removed my shoes and stretched out on the soft mat. I watched a few other climbers work around a bouldering problem with an arduous seated start—some of the climbers were unable to even get off the ground, but they stayed doggedly at it in successive attempts. I recalled reading what Wills had said regarding his successful Wetterhorn ascent: "It was nervous work; a good head, a stout heart, a steady hand and foot were needed." Not a bad way to think about climbing, but also not a bad way to think about the grander context.

Alfred Wills 1828-1912, English Climber, Alpine Club President 1864-5, at his chalet, The Eagles' Nest, above Sixt, France
Photo Courtesy of the Alpine Club Photo Library, London

8 What we talk about when we talk about bouldering

When I was in high school, the only climbing gym in town was a warehouse-like facility that shared its rent with an amateur gymnastics club. In order to reach the gym's climbing walls, one first had to amble past a display of gymnastics trophies, a surplus of tumbling mats, a balance beam, a springboard and more often than not a troupe of nimble gymnasts bouncing through practice routines. On the surface, this seemed like an odd pairing—shaggy-haired dirtbags like me practicing dynos alongside gymnasts gunning for artistic team medals. In fact, having the climbers and the gymnasts converging under a single roof was merely a coincidence. However, as I would discover years later, climbing and gymnastics aren't as far apart as the respective clientele back in those days would have led one to believe. Some similarities are obvious—the control of one's center of gravity on an inanimate object, for starters. But a shared heritage between the two crafts is also present.

The connection between climbing and gymnastics goes something like this: Climbing kinesthesis in modern times, post-Wills, post-Hillary, and post-all other generations, is directly related to the popularity of bouldering—particularly the perpetuation of astronomically challenging single-move or double-move bouldering-style sequences. This was exemplified when Dan took up an exercise regime of bouldering problems to improve his performance on the much-longer route *Columbus*. But bouldering, as its own, autonomous pursuit, actually owes its existence and its initial aesthetic to gymnastics more so than to mountaineering.

No man is more closely tied to this union of gymnastics and bouldering than John Gill. While climbing on boulders had been around for centuries as a way of playful training, it was Gill who had the vision in the 1950s to make the recreation a free-standing discipline. In Gill's eyes, bouldering didn't have to be relegated to a form of training for longer, roped-up climbs. On the contrary, bouldering offered plenty of challenges and nuances—and necessitated far less hardware than mountain climbing.

An adolescent in post-World War II America, Gill started climbing shortly before he entered college. This was the same era when Jack Kerouac and the Beat Generation were citing Zen as an influence on their literature, and Eastern philosophic concepts were being applied to a growing number of American fields. Thus, it was fitting that Gill thought to take a similarly interdisciplinary approach to climbing. "When I started thinking about bouldering as meditation in the 1950s, I don't recall anyone else sharing my ideas," Gill said when I posed questions to him about the many influences of early bouldering. "Of course, there were only a few boulderers around then. I was getting into yoga and Zen, experimenting, and I was also developing gymnastic abilities on my own."

The gymnastics correlation is noteworthy because it likely wouldn't have materialized had it not been for a gymnastics class that Gill was required to take in college. "I enrolled at Georgia Tech and began a gymnastics course required for all graduates," Gill said. "I was clueless about the sport, and long and lanky as well, but it really appealed to me. After that first year—1954—I was climbing the rope for speed and doing a little on the rings as well with the Georgia Tech gymnastics squad from time to time."

Gill transferred to the University of Georgia in 1956 and met a few other "displaced gymnasts" who, like Gill, had an interest in gymnastics but were not involved in the strict, high-level competitive tiers of the sport. The students formed their own university gymnastics club and met a few times a week at the campus gym. Such informality would allow Gill to apply the mechanics and aesthetics of established gymnastics freely to his other passion, rock climbing.

"I thought about other interpretations of artistic

gymnastics and became attracted to the ritual of repetitions, wiring routines and performing them to my own satisfaction," Gill said. "This became a moving meditation for me. And since there were no boulderers in Georgia at the time, I began to perceive bouldering as more an art form and not strictly competitive play, similar to my perception of gymnastics."

John Gill working on the Yellow Wall on a Sylvan Lake Boulder, Black Hills, early 1960s. The dawn of modern bouldering
Photo: John Gill

This merger of the technical with the artistic would be the basis for Gill's earliest perception of bouldering's potential; it could be a discipline that was part skill, but also part expressive performance. "If there had been a number of boulderers around, I might not have gone in that direction," he said. "But, on the other hand, I might not have been attracted to bouldering, relishing it as a solitary pursuit."

The concept of what, exactly, defined recreational climbing had been expanding for a while, even prior to Gill's contributions. Physical fitness, as a component of military training, had been in the spotlight more so than ever before because of the World Wars and the Korean War; activities like rope climbing, scaling walls, and climbing-related obstacle courses had become part of an American soldier's training regime by the mid-1950s. The notion of sport, as a genre, was widening as well. During President Dwight Eisenhower's administration, testing the physical fitness of America's youth became a priority, ushering in an age of increased focus on physical education and peak athletic performance in schools across the country. The President's Challenge, as Eisenhower's broad directive was eventually termed, emphasized the importance of all forms of recreation—indoors as well as outdoors.

Even so, Gill's idea of bouldering didn't immediately catch on with other climbers—those who were still focused on big-wall ascents. Undaunted, he opted to explore the concept largely in his own vision.

One innovation to come out of Gill's early bouldering was the use of hand chalk to improve his grip on the rocks, which was a concept he borrowed directly from gymnastics. But a flashier innovation was the dyno—lunging for hand-holds rather than moving for them in a slow, controlled manner. Nonexistent in the skillsets of mountaineers at the time, dynos—which Gill called free aerials—were rational extensions of gymnastics' use of momentum and sheer muscular force in certain disciplines. "A rope climb begins from a seated position on the floor and a strong pull starts you up, with six or seven strides carrying forth the initial momentum, to the top at 20 feet," he explained. "That first move off the floor is supremely important. The rings also require calculated momentum for the execution of a number of moves—they also demand exceptional strength. So, as I was learning rock climbing on my own in the Deep South, the judicious use of momentum seemed natural."

Gill honed his bouldering moves the following decade, as other American climbers improved their performances and expanded their repertoires of moves on big mountain walls in places like California, New York, Colorado, Wyoming and South Dakota. On the occasions that climbers' paths would cross, however, Gill's bouldering became more of a statement and an inadvertent sales pitch for the burgeoning bouldering discipline. He said, "In the mid-1960s, several of us from various parts of the U.S. would meet in the Black Hills, including Bob Kamps, Dave Rearick, Royal Robbins, Mark Powell, Tom Higgins, Rich Goldsone and others, and Mark Powell once told me that the reason the California climbers treated me with a certain deference was that they respected my physical abilities but I didn't pose a threat to them—bouldering being an enjoyable but ultimately trivial activity. When I began soloing short climbs of high difficulty—particularly the Thimble [in South Dakota's Black Hills] in 1961, which was probably the first 5.12—a number of more traditional climbers began to have second thoughts about bouldering."

Bouldering developed a buzz and expanded to numerous climbing circles. Then, in the early 1970s, bouldering caught on with the Stonemasters, a group of accomplished climbers around Yosemite—and Gill realized that the discipline he had modernized just 15 years earlier had taken on a life of its own. "John Long and John Bachar, fresh and dewy-eyed, like young Greek gods, showed up in Pueblo, Colorado, and I took them on a little tour of the local rocks, particularly a couple of projects I had saved for them," Gill recalled. "In their performances and their talent, I caught a glimpse of the future."

The increase in bouldering's popularity was not without modifications to Gill's original vision. Artistry gradually became less of an analytic consideration, as technicality and physical challenge became the main gauges used by most boulderers when assessing a given problem. "From the beginning of my bouldering career, I can't think of anyone who seriously shared my perception of bouldering as a gymnastic routine, to be polished and enjoyed, regardless of difficulty," Gill reflected. "There were other climbers who were very smooth on the little rocks—Rich Goldstone, for one—but didn't think of graceful performance as on a par with difficulty."

Ultimately, bouldering developed into a form that saw

a problem's degree of difficulty as the sole metric, which is the paradigm that bouldering still utilizes to this day.

Gill moved to Pueblo, Colorado, in the early 1970s, and worked as a mathematician and math professor. He had been drawn to climbing partly due to its exercise component and its individualism, but he had also been attracted to a novelty aspect that was disappearing in bouldering by the 1970s and '80s.

"I continued to put up moderate bouldering problems in the area, exploring the cliffs and outcrops within an hour's drive from Pueblo, and particularly exploring new climbs on granite domes and towers at Hardscrabble Pass, spending many happy days there putting up exploratory free-solo routes and repeating them," Gill said. "I was no longer terribly interested in pushing myself on boulders, being over 40 years old, although I liked to play around on the little rocks."

Gill was not bitter about any of bouldering's permutations, but he acknowledged that the contemporary discipline varies significantly from his original idea. The act of highballing—bouldering to exceptionally tall heights—for example, was, in some ways, also a result of bouldering's popularity boom. Gill said, "As more and more people took up climbing, it became more difficult to achieve favorable recognition unless some boundaries were pushed. If you had topped out a specific difficulty level, one way to move ahead of the pack was to risk more."

This is not to imply that artistry went completely extinct in regards to modern bouldering and climbing. Gill continued to climb in his own style throughout the 1990s and into the 2000s. A torn bicep at age 50 derailed his climbing for a while, but the long recovery process allowed him to revisit many of his earlier boulders with accumulated wisdom from decades as an imaginative practitioner, a veritable artist of climbing. "I gave up any attempt to push bouldering at that time, and rather spent more time on longer, fairly easy solo climbs I had explored and established, both near Pueblo and further north in central Wyoming and the Tetons, returning there for several summers, soloing climbs I had done in the late 1950s," he said. "The years from age 50 to age 70 were the most enjoyable in my climbing life."

One could argue that the artistic quality actually became paramount as photographs and videos—those media that visually documented climbing as art—developed in the decades that followed Gill's earliest contributions. But those media entailed an observer making climbing into a subject; it was different than the craft itself being the creative endeavor—or being a form of meditation, as Gill had articulated. Nonetheless, interviewing John Gill had emphasized bouldering's early duality, equal parts poetic and athletic, and my correspondence with him had laid some groundwork for a closer examination of modern climbing's visual aesthetic.

John Gill perfecting one of his dynamic moves on stone in
Pennyrile Forest, Kentucky
Photo: John Gill

9 | Climbing in the
Digital Age

If the blossoming of the Internet Age and the subsequent puberty of all-things-digital has brought anything to the world of climbing, it's the abundance of climbing videos now available with a couple clicks of the mouse, a few taps on the tablet screen. I remembered growing up in the Dark Ages before video-sharing and personal uploading, and it wasn't pretty. As a young teenager, if I wanted to watch an astounding climb, options were limited to a handful of hard-to-find VHS tapes—early volumes of Eric Perlman's *Masters of Stone* series might ring a bell to some readers, or the forgotten and campy Clint Eastwood feature-length action film from 1975, *The Eiger Sanction*.

In my apartment in Seoul, while fending off bouts of stir-craziness amid the humidity, I tried to imagine the climbing community operating nowadays with such limited access to videos and digital clips of the sport, and it felt on par with trying to imagine a literature scholar without easy access to a basic library. When perusing the Internet's video highlights of climbing that have popped up in recent years, one thing becomes clear: A new generation of climbers has emerged and vaulted the sports' possibilities into the stratosphere. Thankfully many of the extraordinary feats of those climbers have been recorded and will likely be enjoyed onscreen for generations to come.

Nothing exemplifies this more than watching an Internet video of a phenom named Ashima Shiraishi send V12- and V13-level bouldering problems in Hueco Tanks, Texas—bouldering problems so technically difficult that they would have been incomprehensible just a couple of decades ago. Shiraishi traverses the stark inclines with near-infinitesimal hand crimps and expert foot movement, smiling and laughing the whole time like she's a child on a playground. Of course, it's not that much of an exaggeration, as Shiraishi was only 10 years old at the time of the video.

Zooey Ahn, a powerful Korean climber and a cook whose pancake recipe should be world famous, shared my addiction to passing hours watching climbing videos on lazy afternoons. So, deciding to make the most of a rest day, I invited Zooey over to help me compile something of an ultimate visual playlist of modern climbing high spots.

It seemed fitting to start by watching videos of Lynn Hill, since Zooey looked up to Hill as an inspiration, and I had been captivated by Hill ever since I read a book about her climbing ability years ago.

American rock climbing had been steadily expanding on the public's radar since the Golden Age of Yosemite climbing in the 1960s, but it was Lynn Hill's appreciation for sport climbing tradition, as well as incredible command for pushing the envelope, that made her arguably the first rock star of the sport in the 1980s. The celebrity buzz peaked with a record-setting 1993 free climb of *The Nose* on El Capitan in Yosemite, and again in her self-one-upsmanship the following year when she repeated the climb in a single day. In old video clips from the climbs that have fortunatey been transferred to the modern infinity of cyberspace, Hill works methodically and calmly—you'd never guess she's in the midst of completing a climb that nobody else in history had done at the time.

From legendary video clips of Hill, Zooey and I moved somewhat backwards to video clips of pioneers Boone Speed and German superstar Wolfgang Güllich powering up routes in the distressingly undocumented (on video, at least) 1980s, and then we skipped ahead to clips of climbers of the mid-1990s. Zooey and I munched on palm-sized pancakes and sat in awe of a video clip of Tommy Caldwell and Kevin Jorgeson connecting sections of *The Dawn Wall* on El Capitan in Yosemite. Caldwell and Jorgeson would eventually complete their project on January 14, 2015, after spending seven years working intermittently on the route's 32 pitches. The freeing of *The Dawn Wall*, completing the route by using gear only as a safety precaution, would turn out to be a stupendous achievement. It was documented with all forms of modern communication, including cell phone videos, photos in national news outlets and quotidian social media updates. There was a live online stream for viewers to watch the completion of the route's final four pitches. President Barack Obama even congratulated Caldwell and Jorgeson on the first free ascent of the wall, and superlatives abounded about an old-time spirit of adventure being brought back into the world.

Anyone looking for a *Rocky*-style rousing story in climbing certainly doesn't need to look any further than the life and times of Tommy Caldwell. Originally from Estes Park, Colorado, Caldwell's love of climbing was instilled in him at an early age by his father, whom he climbed with frequently as a youngster. In 1995, Caldwell entered the International Sport Climbing Championship competition in Snowbird, Utah, in the Citizens division—essentially the division for casual climbers, laypersons and amateurs. An unknown at the time but undoubtedly possessing the indubitable eye of the tiger that would eventually make him a modern legend, he won the division's competition and subsequently entered the main division, where the competition was much steeper and far more legitimate. Undaunted and unintimidated by making it to the big-time, Caldwell climbed hard and won the main division at Snowbird as well, and in the process firmly cemented himself as a new force in the climbing world.

From there, the story turns more to a thriller narrative, and includes Caldwell getting captured by armed terrorists—and escaping—while climbing in Kyrgyzstan in 2000, and also gruesomely losing part of a finger in a sawing accident a year later. Such an injury would permanently sideline most climbers for the remainder of their wall-hanging careers, but Caldwell continues to send climbs at the elite level and be a tiresome ambassador for the sport in various media outlets to this day.

Zooey took a break from the videos to re-grease the frying pan over the stove and pour a viscous line of pancake batter into a perfect disc shape in the pan's center. The batter popped and sputtered, and then settled into its aromatic sizzle. Shortly after that, I slid the golden-brown pancake onto my plate and took a bite—so fluffy that it was the palatable embodiment of a lazy summer.

We managed to while away a couple more hours watching videos of Canadian climber Sean McColl work a renowned route called *Dreamcatcher* in the Canadian climbing mecca of Squamish, British Columbia, American boulderer Daniel Woods crush various problems in an indoor American Bouldering Series competition, and ferociously driven Adam Ondra of the Czech Republic rocket up outdoor overhangs in Céüse, France. We watched a clip of Sasha DiGiulian climbing a route rated 5.14d in the Red River Gorge called *Pure Imagination*; upon completion of the route in 2011, she became the first American woman to check off such a difficult grade.

We came then to videos of professional climber Chris Sharma. We watched footage of Sharma successfully completing a route that was widely considered to be rated 5.15 in the summer of 2001. Then known as *Biographie*, and also located in the crag of Céüse, France, more than six hours south of Paris, the 120-foot route had been set more than a decade before Sharma finally sent it.

Sharma's accomplishment on the long-established climb, which he consequently renamed *Realization*, sent shock waves through the climbing world. Like the public's collective mindset about running a mile in less than four minutes prior to Roger Bannister's feat in 1954, some people in the climbing community had long thought that completing any route rated 5.15 (or 9a+ under the French rating system) would simply be beyond the capabilities of human mechanics. But in the video footage of Sharma's first ascent, which originally appeared in a climbing DVD series known as *Dosage* before being further immortalized on the Internet, Sharma is shown managing to fit two and three fingers up to their first knuckle into tiny, well-chalked stone pockets. He moves painstakingly up the blue- and beige-colored vertical face in successive big-reach moves. He completes the upper crux with a propulsive dead-point—flawlessly executing his airborne surge to secure a grip on a diminutive handhold at the peak of his upward movement. After that, the route gets progressively more leisurely— at least for a climber of Sharma's caliber—although no doubt still mentally taxing. "I think the best attitude for me to have on this [route] is just, 'When it's the right time to do it, I'll do it,'" a young-faced, bright-eyed Sharma says in the video.

"And I guess every other time that I don't do it, it just wasn't the right time; it wasn't meant to be."

I recall going to the local indoor climbing gym near my home shortly after Sharma's epic send of *Realization* in 2001, after word had spread, the news had been publicized, and the comprehension was starting to set in that the supposed 5.15 barrier had just been decimated in one fell swoop. Everyone, even the most casual of climbers, was talking about Sharma, raving about his ascent. It was as if a new era of climbing had begun as a result of Sharma's flawless deadpoint.

What often gets overlooked is the timing of Sharma's *Realization*. Lynn Hill had become a celebrity in the climbing community as a result of her accomplishments, and a climber named Dan Goodwin had garnered news headlines in the 1980s for scaling several of the tallest skyscrapers of the day—the Sears Tower and the John Hancock Center among them—in a superhero costume.

But Sharma's ascent of *Realization* placed him not only at the top of the sport and in the news, but also on the cusp of the digital communication boom. Simply put, more people could become aware of Sharma and his successive feats than ever possible with the clunky media and sluggish communicative interaction of the 1980s and '90s. Almost overnight, Sharma, the introspective 20-year-old from Santa Cruz, California, represented not only climbing, but also the broad and burgeoning market of "extreme sports," to the world. ESPN's X Games, the main media showcase for such endeavors, was in full swing at that point. Additionally, climbing websites were sprouting up on the Internet with increasing frequency, and rather opportunely, indoor climbing walls were popping up in gyms and on college campuses across the country. Climbing was precipitously hip, and it was seen as the alternative to the glossy mainstream sports like baseball, football and basketball.

Years later, Sharma would cite the personal and liberating aspects of climbing as some of the act's most unique qualities, and he would note that climbing is an activity that can be performed virtually anywhere that there is a mountain or wall. Furthermore, Sharma asserted that there is no such thing as winning or losing at climbing—there is only climbing.

Nothing exemplified that concept more, or made it more appealing to the general public, than Sharma scrupulously working on *Realization* halfway across the world in 2001 and inspiring countless new, young climbers to hop on a wall and test their own personal limits.

An afternoon of video clips and homemade pancakes resulted in Zooey wanting to get outside and climb, even if it was only for a fraction of an hour before the sun sank and the dim light of dusk lumbered in. So, we said goodbye to our intended rest day. We headed outdoors, bouldered and reclined on soft mats, and then found a Rasta-themed dive bar where a small road arched around a line of new apartment buildings on the edge of the neighborhood. We ordered tall beers and snacked on almonds with our minds still on the videos, particularly Sharma's *Realization*. There have been more difficult routes sent over the years, and other climbers have since repeated *Realization*. Sharma has since moved on from being the young wunderkind of extreme sports to being granted inevitable statesman-of-climbing status. He owns his own gym, Sender One, in Southern California, and he has started a nonprofit organization—the Sharmafund—that introduces children to climbing. But he still maintains the same mental drive, the same kinship with the rocks that got him to the dance in the first place.

"You try something that is way above your level and it requires a huge amount of dedication," he said in an interview with *Climbing* magazine. "In those situations, that's when I feel the best. I feel like I'm living my purpose in my life. If I have a project that really motivates me, everything is perfectly clear. There is no confusion about what I should be doing. Everything is obvious. I'm here trying this project, that's what I'm here to do. I need to find things that push me mentally and physically to my ultimate level."

I was light years away from Sharma's athletic accomplishments, obviously—just a writer sipping foamy beer to reggae tunes on a humid summer evening. Nevertheless, a climber is a climber, and big accomplishments are irrelevant in the larger scheme of affinities and predilections; in that way, I knew exactly the type of purpose Sharma was talking about. I felt it too.

Chris Sharma, inarguably one of the most important figures
in modern climbing
Photo: Corey Rich/ Aurora Photos

10 | Other ways of
seeing the sea cliffs

Zen Buddhism asserts that a man's mind provides much of the struggle in life and that fear originates from the mind. In Christianity, the Bible urges man to submit his anxieties to God, as man is ultimately a being of benevolence, not fear. The Bhagavad Gita, a renowned Hindu scripture, implies that fear and desire both emerge from the same place in one's psyche. Such sweeping decrees can be useful, but it is also sensible to aim the age-old concept of unease at the distinct referent of climbing. Author David Roberts, for example, is more specific when writing about what keeps climbers attentive and striving to maintain control: "You could never stay bored: The risk alone keeps your synapses jangling."

Whether viewed through a religious lens or resulting from an ever-present fear of failure—that is, a fear of falling—control and composure are vital to movement on rocks, and a drop in either of those creates problems at a blistering rate. This is all heightened for someone when crashing ocean waves and jagged basalt rocks are added to the equation, as they were one day when Dan and Zooey and I decided to climb sea cliffs on the southern Korean island of Jeju.

Formed by volcanic activity, Jeju has a subtropical aura that makes it feel in many ways like a Southeast Asian tourist hideaway more than part of temperate South Korea. Palm trees, fresh citrus sold from roadside stands, beaches rife with layabouts and surf bums—Jeju has a way of making the rest of the world fade away in typical island style. Once one heads past the coastal hotels and the tourist crunch, however, things get welcomingly rugged.

The sea cliffs of South Korea's Jeju Island
Photo: Dan Kojetin

Dan, Zooey and I met up with another group of climbers at the top of the gray, forehead-like cliff that jutted out over the sea. Far below, dark green and blue hues in the ocean water sparkled and tumbled in serrated waves. Lumpy boulders loomed as enormous dark blotches beneath the water's surface. Dan said that we were very close to an active Buddhist temple, and occasionally while climbing at the sea cliffs in the past, he'd seen monks meditating on top of some of the rocks.

On the cliff's edge, our group prepared for a rappel far down to the base of the cliff, where there was a small patch of flat stone to serve as a suitable belay spot.

"The choice is either rappel down or hike far around the cliff and then down some nasty rocks," Dan said and noted that he'd seen other climbers get scared stiff at the thought of rappelling into the abyss of exploding waves and sea-salt mist. "It can feel a little sketchy," he cautioned us.

Everyone in our group was capable of successfully completing the rappel if composure and control could be maintained. But to Dan's point, the sensory overload of jagged cliffs and noisy waves, along with a steep roped descent to a petite belay rock, did have the potential to be overwhelming.

And that's exactly what happened when one of the young women in our group decided that perhaps she had bitten off more than she could chew. She took a few minutes at the top of the cliff to assess the scene—to buffer her anxiety against a realistic assessment of her abilities. She then began to cry, and with tears streaming down her face, she conferred with her boyfriend and eventually decided to try the sea cliffs some other day. With that, our group split up: A few people went to climb the sea cliffs, while the rest of us—Dan, Zooey and myself included—took to a leafy knoll a few dozen feet from the edge of the cliff. We found a shady spot beneath some pines and dug into our picnic quesadillas. There was a stray beige dog wandering the area, its ribs poking against its tight skin and dirty fur. We figured the dog had been long forgotten or sadly abandoned by other picnickers. We took a liking to it—Zooey fed it scraps from our bucket of caramel popcorn and chased it around the tall grass.

Dan and I used a couple of carabiners to set up a high slackline between two palm trees under the pretext that slacklining would improve our balance for climbing. In fact, if the slackline was any indication, I had the balance skills of a drunken rhinoceros: At first I couldn't even stand on the tight webbing—much less balance in momentary stillness and walk on it—without the aid of Dan and Zooey.

Zooey was far more proficient on the line than I was. Even a broken toe that had hindered her climbing for a week didn't stop her from standing up on the line and balancing with more grace than my wobbly, pathetic display. The real standout, however, was the young woman who had been afraid to rappel from the sea cliffs. She walked along the slackline with ease, and she even carried on a conversation with the rest of us while balancing on one foot. It turned out that she owned a slackline and practiced often on it around Jeju. She assured me that I would improve quickly with practice, although I couldn't imagine ever making the gains that would bring me up to her level. Still, I appreciated her vote of confidence.

When one of the climbers from the other group had had enough of scaling the sea cliffs and getting sunburned on the exposed, wave-bombarded belay rock, he topped out and joined us under the pines. We all ate a lunch of hummus, cucumbers and quesadillas in the shade.

"How was the climbing?" Zooey asked him.

His cheeks and nose were burned bright red, practically glowing from the scorching sun in the midday, cloudless sky.

"It was a lot of fun, but I'm soaked," he said and showed us his wet shirt. "There were a couple of times when big waves broke against the rocks while I was belaying and got me all wet."

He tried the slackline as well—another apparent professional tightrope walker in our midst. He did turns and practically pirouetted on the thin line.

At one point, Dan and I were talking while other people were laughing and tossing food scraps to the friendly stray dog. I asked Dan about the Buddhist monks he'd seen meditating on the cliffs. Then I jokingly asked if the monks ever rock climbed.

"No, not here on the sea cliffs," he said. He paused. "But I did go bouldering with a monk once at another place in Korea. He was awesome—every time he'd mess up, he'd get so mad and yell at the rock."

There seemed to be something very non-monk-like in that image, the concept of a supremely calm man being so overcome with frustration at the failure of a minute handhold or foothold. Yet, on the other hand, yelling at something supremely inanimate—a rock—seemed all too Zen; the venting of the self toward something that had no mind or self, and in that sense, represented a conceptual ideal.

When our picnic far above the crashing ocean waves was finished and the stray dog had moved on cheerfully to another group of friendly picnicking strangers, we unclipped the slackline and packed up our food scraps.

We hiked down to a cove where a deep pool of water was enveloped by tall stone towers. Zooey dubbed the place *Rock and Roll*, on account of its positioning among the cliffs and its lolling blue waves. We decided to go for a swim. We climbed a 15-foot rock, from which we could jump and plunge into the sun-warmed saltwater below. We swam and relaxed on the hot rocks for more than an hour. Before we left, I asked Dan if he was bummed that we hadn't climbed at all that day.

"No way," he said. "Just being here is the best." With that, he tilted back his head and backstroked into the blue horizon of the ocean, surrounded by towering cliff ledges, dwarfed by wisps of white cloud far overhead.

11 | Climbing and ethical responsibility

While resting a throbbing finger, the ligament searing from hanging off a two-finger pocket for too long on an overhanging route the previous day, I decided to use the downtime to peruse various climbing obituaries—not exactly the most joyful literature for casual reading, but the obituaries satiated my never-ending appetite for learning about famed and forgotten climbers from the past.

Sport climbing being as relatively young as it is, we are fortunate to have most of the first generation of great climbers—the pioneers of the techniques used today—still around and capable of commenting on the evolution of the sport. The sad flipside of that is that when one of the craft's forefathers passes away, it's a monumental loss, and the remaining large fraternity of pioneers is left to reflect on it, left to bereave together and dwell on the absence. I came across obituaries from a number of climbers from the 1940s and '50s who set the bar—and raised the bar—on mountains around the world, and I read the praises bestowed upon them by their peers. However, it was an obituary of legendary big-wall hanger Warren Harding that particularly caught my eye. I had only vaguely known about Harding—he was as a landmark name in climbing history, a champion of a bygone era, and his fondness for wine was renowned. But that was about all I knew.

As it turns out, as much as Harding had a reputation for hedonism—for imbibing and keeping a fittingly social campground—and as much as he has remained a symbol of the alternative 1960s sports culture, he was first and foremost a bold, adventurous climber. He began climbing in the mid-20th Century, and by the end of the millennium had dozens of landmark first ascents to his credit. The most notable of those ascents was *The Nose* on El Capitan in Yosemite. The tale of

Harding's first ascent there would become legendary among climbers due mainly to the stories of Harding and his climbing partners working diligently throughout the nights on the mountain, in the midst of biting autumn cold, and eventually reaching the peak after nearly two weeks on the rock in 1958.

Warren Harding, one of the most accomplished climbers of his day, and a man whose abilities and character would inadvertently contribute to the lasting dirtbag archetype
Photo: Glen Denny

In many ways, the image of Harding grinding out *The Nose* ascent would help give American climbing a boost of credibility on the international scene, as it harkened back to tales of grizzled, intrepid European mountaineers fighting the elements to get up mountains at all costs in the previous centuries.

And Harding was just getting started, in terms of his tenacity and acclaim. Twenty years after his first ascent of *The Nose*, he and a fellow climber would be stymied on El Capitan's southeast face due to heavy rain. They would be rescued amid high publicity, only to press on another time and eventually ascend the route at a later date.

Of course, in the midst of all the climbing, Harding's embrace of the good life—celebrating his ascents with alcohol and revelry—served to elevate the public's fascination with his persona. Harding was, in that way, a stark contrast to several of the other famed American climbers of the era, and especially to the more technically sound Royal Robbins. In an interview, Harding would say of Robbins, "We were bumping heads everywhere, vying for first ascents."

All the attention and press about Harding's climbing supposedly resulted in talks about a possible movie based on his life and rivalry with Robbins, and also afforded him a steady circuit of giving lectures and speeches for much of the remainder of his life.

Royal Robbins, a contemporary of Harding's who also earned recognition and accolades for his accomplishments in Yosemite

Photo: Glen Denny

Something that gets largely overlooked in discussions on Harding's contributions during sport climbing's infancy is his unintended role in merging climbing with environmentalism. Harding was known for the widespread placement of artificial bolts in the walls that he climbed—a practice that, along with tactics other climbers occasionally adopted such as carving and chipping handholds and footholds into the stone and drilling a superfluous amount of holes into the rocks, permanently changed the natural structure of routes and essentially defaced the mountain faces, but were nonetheless more acceptable during his era. A debate of whether or not such intentional modification of the stone was ethical gained steam and flourished for years.

Harding, being as hard-nosed as you'd expect from a guy who had endured hypothermia and a number of injuries in the name of his climbing, doggedly defended his bolt-placement practices, which only served to elevate the debate to an even larger audience. What resulted was widespread critical thinking about matters of environmentalism in the climbing community.

In the end, it was minimal-impact climbing that prevailed as the modus operandi on the mountains for a vast majority of climbers of all skill levels. Chipping away bits of rock in order to accommodate one's need for a suitable handhold or foothold is now seen as one of the biggest transgressions in the sport—and it's also illegal in most regions—but one cannot read about Harding without realizing the role he played in spurring dialogue on the topic.

Jumping off from the subjects of drilling and carving climbing holds, climbing's environmental consciousness seeped into a number of other causes, in a sort of natural progression of highland stewardship brought about by the bolt placement debate of the 1960s and '70s. The Access Fund, a nonprofit organization based out of Colorado, began in 1991 with the aim of preserving natural land for climbers. The Honnold Foundation, started by Alex Honnold in 2012, supports and advocates various causes linked with sustainability, solar energy and other intelligent concepts around the world. Gear companies with international offices like Black

Diamond Equipment have taken stances on the subjects of fair labor and environmental sustainability in regard to their brands. John Ellison's founding of Climbers Against Cancer in early 2013, as well as Michael Cumming's founding of Operation Climb On for military veterans in 2013, proved that climbing's popularity can be used effectively for worthwhile causes that reside beyond the ecological realm. Similarly, Climbing Toward Confidence, an offshoot program of North Carolina-based OurVoice, uses climbing as a teaching tool to improve the confidence and self-assurance of teenage girls. And Yosemite climber Yvon Chouinard, a contemporary of Warren Harding's, saw that the Patagonia company backed a slew of conservation causes ranging from recycling of clothing materials to extensive freshwater cleanup.

In an interview with *Sierra* magazine, however, Chouinard asserted that conservation, and change on any substantial scale, owes to the grunt work of individuals rather than big business policy. "If you think about all the gains our society has made, from independence to now, it wasn't government, it was activism," Chouinard said. "People think, 'Oh, Teddy Roosevelt established Yosemite National Park, what a great president.' BS. It was John Muir who invited Roosevelt out and then convinced him to ditch his security and go camping. It was Muir, an activist, a single person."

Switching to other regions of the country, the year 2003 saw two devoted Midwestern climbers, Liz and Rick Weber, purchase 350 acres of land in Kentucky's Red River Gorge. Known as the Muir Valley, the Weber's newly acquired chunk of real estate was solely preserved in order to develop the land's multitude of climbing opportunities. But on a broader scale, the Weber's purchase proved that land and wilderness conservation could be fostered by small-town folks as much as by leading businesses.

Two years later, in 2005, the Carolina Climbers Coalition made a similarly minded purchase in a different part of the country. Largely fueled by monetary donations from climbers domestically and internationally, the coalition bought the most expansive vertical rock face in the eastern United States, Laurel Knob, near Cashiers, North Carolina, and made it accessible to the climbing public. And conserva-

*Climbing in the Red River Gorge made possible in
large part by the conservation efforts of Liz and Rick Weber*
Photo: Andy Wickstrom www.wickstromphoto.com

tion coalitions in other parts of the country have made comparable land acquisitions since then.

In a way, it was appropriate that my day of finger ligament rest and environmentalism review culminated in listening to Dan talk about his graduate school thesis to me as we downed microwaved dumplings on the screened-porch snack bar of a hole-in-the-wall convenience store on a humid night. Dan's academic research was in the field of public administration, but he was hoping to use it as a base for working on environmental causes—ideally issues that affect climbers. "That would be one way to turn public administration into something that's not so boring," he said.

What was propelling Dan into the dreadful desk sector of outdoor adventure was the ongoing conundrum of woodland and mountainous areas having to develop for profits—catering to tourists and businesses—while also maintaining the ruggedness and remoteness that draws the tourists and outdoorsmen to them in the first place.

The issue of land conservation versus development

has long been one of the main battles for climbers, who have lived in fear that someday their sacred crags will become freeways, mini-marts or gaudy resorts. Worse still is the threat that climbers' precious mountain areas and consecrated crags will remain rugged and remote and undeveloped, and yet the very act of climbing them will be deemed illegal.

"Climbing was almost banned in the national parks in the U.S. a few years ago," Dan said. "That would have been such a bad deal because that would have included places like Joshua Tree or Yosemite Valley—arguably the best climbing in the U.S., and maybe the world."

Dan was referring to the fact that the previous spring had seen the director of the U.S. National Park Service, Jonathan Jarvis, declare that the use of a modest amount of fixed climbing anchors inserted into the rocks—which encompasses a majority of the climbing routes in the United States—was officially legal, as long as it was done with approval from the local park authorities. Until that time, climbers around the United States were scaling walls in an opaque fog of authorization, unsure of when and where an all-out ban on fixed anchors might occur. The U.S. Forest Service had even gone so far as to ban fixed anchors in certain federal land areas in 1998.

Worst case scenario, climbers would be forced to either give up climbing altogether on all federal land, or continue to pursue their vertical ambitions only in secret and in illegality. Such is the current fate of BASE jumpers, who sneak into national parks and parachute from steep cliffs—hoping simply to get in, have fun and then get off the land without detection by park officials.

In the end, a balance for climbers was agreed upon thanks to advocacy work by the Access Fund and other groups. Bolted anchors got the thumbs up from the U.S. National Park Service, but with the caveat that additional authorization might be needed.

Dan and I scraped the noodles from our bowls and walked outside to his motorcycle. Nearby, a group of kids was kicking a soccer ball in the darkness, laughing as they stumbled blindly into each other. Dan clipped on his bike helmet and gave the engine a growling rev, then gathered one more thought about where his graduate school studies could take him.

"The key is always finding a balance, right?" Dan said. "Climbing doesn't really add much monetary value to a place. It doesn't bring in a lot of money. So the question is: What value does climbing add to a place? I'd like to help developers and conservationists answer that question."

12 | A more significant sanctuary of existence

Staring at the vast night sky, an indigo expanse dotted with star clusters and the low light of the moon, it was easy to think with a wide scope and let small thoughts swell to grand proportions. I relaxed in a camping chair with a view of a rocky crag silhouetted ahead of me, the scent of a nearby hibiscus patch wafting across the grass. The hibiscus flowers signify eternity in some Eastern lore, just as the stars in the celestial night have long epitomized the everlasting unknown to outdoorsmen, vagabonds and wanderers in the West. As much as one can try to simply enjoy the backcountry darkness and hugeness for what it is, it's also impossible for a climber, at some point in an ongoing string of crags and routes and bouldering problems, not to consider the distinct aspect of the pursuit that lies in a nebulous state of being—neither physical nor mental, but a more significant sanctuary of existence.

It's possible to over-spiritualize anything, but I also felt that most climbers I'd met found the joys of the craft not in, say, landing a sick four-points-off dyno or on-sighting the crux of a V14 boulder problem (although God bless those who are so endowed). Such feats are impressive but eventually forgotten. Even Dan and Zooey, when I posed the question to them one evening near a rocky beach, had a hard time recalling which single moves of the previous day had left them feeling most psyched.

"I don't know," said Dan. "I'm just glad at this point to be getting big calluses back on my hands."

The delight, then, lies in aspects that reverberate deeper and more enduringly than the jaw-dropping displays of kinesthesis-on-stone. And of all the men and women who have attempted to swathe climbing in some metaphysical cloth, very few command attention or have seen climbing bifurcated so significantly into the glorious and the horrific like photographer and multi-discipline climber Craig DeMartino.

DeMartino was involved in a serious climbing accident in 2000 on serriformed Lumpy Ridge in Rocky Mountain National Park. Following a miscommunication with a belay partner, DeMartino, who was clinging to the top of a 100-foot route, fell to the ground. While a free-fall from such a great height would kill most people, the fact that DeMartino landed on his feet indubitably saved his life. However, the compression effect of having such velocity absorbed by the bones of his feet, legs and back also proved catastrophic.

Upon impact, DeMartino obliterated the bones of his feet and ankles—in an illuminating example of the immense force of the fall, the bottoms of DeMartino's climbing shoes burst apart when his feet touched down. He suffered a broken back, broken neck, broken ribs, broken elbow, punctured lung and ruptured leg arteries, and had to endure a five-hour evacuation from the spot of the fall without anesthesia. He was alive, but barely.

In the ensuing days and weeks, doctors operated on DeMartino multiple times, but it remained unlikely that he would ever walk again, much less live any semblance of an active daily routine and enjoy the outdoor recreations to which he had previously been accustomed. But DeMartino defied the odds—something he would do repeatedly—and eventually regained functional mobility in both legs thanks to rigorous physical therapy, first in an assisted living facility and then from his home in Colorado.

One of the most surprising addendums in DeMartino's ongoing recuperation was that he didn't develop any resentment toward climbing; he maintained an interest in climbing—or at least an ember of curiosity—in part because many of his friends were avid climbers, and thus he remained always on the periphery of the sport during his long road to recovery. "For me, being a task-oriented person, when a doctor or physical therapist told me what I needed to do to get out of bed, walk, climb, whatever it was, I was able to focus on that goal," DeMartino said when I reached out to him to explain the challenges of his recovery. "At first, you are dealing with the question, 'Who am I after the accident?' Once you start to figure that out, you begin to explore what your new 'normal' looks like. I wasn't sure if I wanted to climb again, but I wanted to make that choice and not have the accident make it for me as it had done with so many other things. In the end, it came down to me being curious about what my new body could actually do."

However, despite DeMartino's drive, doctors said he would certainly never climb again, and he encountered a major setback a year and a half after the accident when he began to develop intense, persistent pain in his right leg. Doctors ruled out an infection, which would have been life-threatening, but the diagnosis wasn't much better: the nerves in DeMartino's leg were essentially on a playback loop, still reacting to the trauma of the 100-foot fall on repeat, and the affliction would only get worse over time.

In reaction to his leg's condition and all the frustrations of the past 18 months, and fed up with having so much of his life controlled and dictated by the accident, DeMartino opted for voluntary amputation of his right leg—an audacious decision, but one that would serve to do away with the surgically patched nerves rather than live the remainder of life exasperated and agonized by them.

Even after the amputation, DeMartino still feels an affinity for climbing, drawn to the release that the body mechanics might provide amid a daily existence of learning to work with his prosthetics.

"Before the accident I had tried other sports, and I still ski and mountain bike a lot," DeMartino told me. "But the feeling of climbing, being alone and solving the problems that climbing throws at you, is really not present in other sports I have tried. I enjoy the movement of climbing, and that, more than anything else about it, was what drew me back. That I get to interact with nature in its raw form is a huge perk as well, but the movement and problem solving aspects of climbing are what keep me doing it."

DeMartino's connection to the walls goes beyond the exercise or the analytical challenges that climbing presents, and he has grown a transcendent gratitude for the climbing life and the fact that it is all-encompassing. "Climbing, for sure, has a deeper impact to me since I got hurt," he said. "Climbing after the accident not only helped my body to heal since it uses every body part, it really helped my mind to heal.

I got to the point of—and continue to be in—more pain than I care to think about, and if I can move it really makes me feel better. The movements I use in climbing help my back to stretch out and relieve some of the pain and joint stiffness. But I also feel like I've really learned a lot about myself with climbing after the accident."

Climbing after the accident, it should be noted, has included checking off an ascent of Yosemite's El Capitan, among other Western hotspots. DeMartino wasn't sure if he wanted to get on big walls again, but he was spurred on by famed climber Hans Florine, widely regarded as one of the fastest climbers of all time. "Hans was the catalyst for me even thinking of wall climbing again, in that he was proposing an 'in a day' approach—which I had never done," DeMartino said. "So I thought, 'I wonder if I can even do that?' And then once I had one climb under my belt, I was curious again if I could do more, which led to climbing *The Nose* of El Capitan in a day, then an All-Disabled Ascent. They were just steps in that progressing curiosity."

Yet, it's not renowned destinations or grueling climbs that inspired DeMartino. "Before the accident, I wanted to be good in order to be the best climber," he said. "Now I am touched by the simple act of climbing and the freedom it gives me. I want to be good at it now simply to be good at it, not for any other reason. And I feel that the search for being good involves me working the craft over my whole lifetime; climbing becomes both a healer and a motivator to keep looking ahead to see what I can do. That makes me whole in many ways, even though I'm not whole physically."

DeMartino was quick to credit not only the healing property of climbing's methodical techniques but also the climbing collective. "My wife, Cyn, and I met in a climbing gym, so climbing has always been a huge part of our lives together," he said. "She is one of the main people in my life that motivates me and makes me want to be better, not just with climbing, but life. I feel that all the people I climb with motivate me in some form: sometimes it's really talented climbers who make me want to try harder, and sometimes it's a first-time climber in one of my clinics who just restores my stoke for climbing in its pure form."

DeMartino's recovery was a testament that climbing had a spiritual side, as capable of providing lasting healing as it was of delivering an instant shot of adrenaline. "Even after 23 years of climbing, it is still my best form of meditation," he said. "I can really be alone with my thoughts when I'm climbing, and I find it's a great form of making my life simple. When I'm climbing, I feel this great sense of calm that I rarely have in my other parts of life."

That meditation—or flow experience that Dr. Rebecca Williams had previously told me about, the singularity of all matters at play on the wall—didn't seem nearly as abstract in light of DeMartino's acknowledgment of its therapeutic benefits.

"When I am climbing, I am truly present," DeMartino said. "If I am above dodgy gear, or on a tall problem, I am not thinking about the bills, my kids' education, or anything other than hitting and holding the next hold. Where else can you have that singular focus and not be criticized for it in today's society?"

He added, "The natural space has always given me the chance to soak up the world and all that was created and continues to be created, as a true observer. It reminds me how small I am, and I think that leads to being a humble human. When you are on the side of El Capitan or a long route somewhere, you see that you are a little speck, and that really spills over into my everyday life. I try to make that a focus—that no matter where I am in life, I'm still that little speck on a wall."

After mulling over that image, being so minute among the vastness, my mind was thinking about the necessity of congregation and cathedral in climbing, moments and places to reflect recurrently, devotedly, on the panorama and everyone's place within it, be it in the vertical or elsewhere. I sat in a camping chair, sipped a drink, and let the crag in my view slip into the full cover of the darkness. I dozed off, and then awoke in the black absolute of midnight, a slight sprinkle of rain in the air, and felt possibly a little more stoke than ever before.

Craig DeMartino finds solace in climbing years after his accident
Photo: Mayah DeMartino

13 | The obligation of experience

There was a night when Dan and I decided that we'd take to the wall for a late climbing session. We met at his apartment at 7:00 in the evening with our gear already packed and ready to go. Dan's girlfriend drove down from a neighboring city to join the outing as well, and Dan dutifully celebrated her long commute by whipping up stir-fried rice and kimchi in a skillet in his kitchen. He served heaping scoops of the hot dish as a pre-climb carbohydrate barrage, and the three of us wolfed down multiple helpings of the spicy mush. Then, in full post-meal comatosis, we sluggishly piled into a car and drove to the most popular night climbing spot.

As we approached the wall, I saw winks of light in the darkness. When we parked and walked closer, I realized that the white blinking lights were headlamps strapped to climbers and belayers. They were tilting their heads in all directions, at all heights on the wall, and working their respective ways up routes in the thick, outdoor darkness.

The wall on a weekday evening was clearly the place to be, a social-recreation nucleus for kids and teenagers from all areas of town. In other towns, in other parts of the world, such a place might be the bleachers of a local field or the cliffs of a quarry—someplace where adolescents can sulk and brood. There didn't seem to be any of that at this hub though, just climbing.

A few of the old-timers of the neighborhood also roamed the space, offering tips, a belay or two, and generally corralling the teenagers and keeping everyone on their best behavior. One of them was a full-faced man named Kyeonghun Oh, commonly referred to simply as Mr. Oh, who had just passed the written exam to be certified as an International Federation of Sport Climbing competition judge. But Mr. Oh's bigger accomplishment, Dan told me, was the establishment of a climbing program at the local high school—and going so far as to install a bouldering gym in the school.

"I wish I had gone to a high school that offered bouldering," Dan said.

As evidenced by the average age of the crowd at the wall, climbing at the school had captivated the teenagers and given them something communal and active to do on languid summer nights. But it had also cultivated and fostered an incredibly adept group of young climbers. At one point, I was standing at the base of a route on the wall and ready to be belayed by Dan when a scrawny, bright-eyed kid asked boldly if he could take my spot—he'd have to go home soon, as the hour was approaching his bedtime, so he wanted to get in one final climb. I was happy to oblige, so I untied and vanquished my position, only to watch the 90-pound string bean glide up the route with relative ease. He dipped his small hands deep into holds that I would have had to crimp with my fingertips.

All climbing spots undoubtedly have their hotshot kids, youths who put the middle-agers and elder climbers to shame. But it was an altogether humbling experience to be surrounded by more than a dozen of such young beasts at one time.

Dan and I stood at the ground and gaped at the proficiency of the next generation of great sport climbers, scaling the wall with lacertilian quickness. At one point, I turned to Dan to see how he was holding up under the spectacle, only to have him turn to me with an enthusiastic and genuine grin. "This is awesome, they're all so good," he said.

He was correct. There was something encouraging about seeing such dominance by the youth. It ensured that the future of climbing as a sport and as a healthy addiction, as well as the perpetuation of difficult routes, was in good hands, albeit hands that just weren't fully grown yet.

Dan and I traded turns cruising up various routes. Dan led a line up a twisting corner of the wall. His girlfriend followed and climbed through shifting headlamp beams and white cones of light from flashlights. She reached the top of the wall in a lattice of shadows. She came back to the ground and we were greeted by a group of kids all wearing identical sweatpants emblazoned with their school's logo.

"Where are you from?" one of the boys asked in

squeaky-voiced salutation.

"I lived in New York for many years before coming to Korea," I said.

He nodded in apparent approval of this fact and then seemed at a loss for words. Talking to me was, I realized, the generational equivalent of the kid talking to his school's principal, so I understood his dumbstruck speechlessness.

"You're a really good climber," I said.

He turned to the wall and gave it a quick up-and-down glance, then shrugged. "I don't think so," he said. "But it's so fun."

I couldn't argue with his succinctness. I gave the boy a chalky high-five as he ran off into the darkness with his buddies, their harnesses and belay devices jingling like sheep bells.

I walked over to Mr. Oh and stood with him for a moment as he looked out over the group. There were at least two dozen teenagers gathered in the night to climb.

"Why do you do it?" I asked Mr. Oh. "Why do you come out here and help all the kids?"

"Young people are the most important part of expanding climbing," he said in broken English. "I started climbing when I was in high school, but I didn't start climbing by myself; I was helped by others. So when I hit 40 years old, I felt like it was my obligation to give my knowledge to new generations."

I turned to say something else to Mr. Oh, but he was gone. He had left the outskirts in a flash and returned to the base of a climb. He was offering a tip about climbing posture and center of gravity to one of the teenagers. It was better, of course, to coach among the players than to coach them from afar.

Once our arms were pumped out, Dan and his girl-friend and I ambled back to our car. A few battery-powered lamps had been set up on the edge of the wall. They gave the climbing space a white luminescence under the clean black sky. The lamps set those people who were within the light apart from the rest of the solid night. It was like the climbing wall was a floating sphere, set distinctly apart from everything around it and all the empty sky so far above it.

14 | What's with the shoes?

As July came to its relaxed, muggy close, and the sidewalks became crowded with tourists and students freed from the academic shackles of summer school, one couldn't help but feel consternations—the realization that the season never slows down enough to be fully appreciated. Soon the days would grow shorter, the nights' swirling breezes slightly chillier, and autumn would begin to intermittently peak its head around the corner.

It was enough to make anyone a little melancholy, or at least shocked at the blazing pace that June and July seemed to possess. One morning, I poured my mug of coffee and realized that, rather than head to the indoor gym for an hour of sunrise bouldering with the gym's manager, my time would be better spent preparing my syllabi for the upcoming fall semester courses that I'd be teaching at the university. I tried my best to shut off the persistent climbing static buzzing in my mind and forced myself to compartmentalize the constant dwelling on handhold sequences, foot movement and fresh air cravings for a substantial chunk of the morning, but it proved to be an arduous task. At lunchtime, I called Zooey and told her shamelessly that I just wished summer could last forever.

"The constant rains are finally finished and now we finally have blue sky, and all you can think about is being bummed out," she said. "That's a weird kind of irony."

She made a good point. And clichéd longing for infinite sunshine and uncluttered, clear days being what they were, there was ultimately no remedy. So, our conversation soon switched to another topic near and dear to climbers: footwear. Zooey needed new climbing shoes, after threading out the seams of her old climbing moccasins. Three years of foot wedging, smearing, toe jamming and heel hooking had finally caught up to the leather and the laces of her favorite pair. After putting in a little more grunt work to prepare for my looming fall semester in academia, I had some free time to join her on her quest for new shoes.

People who have never laced up a pair of climbing shoes might not know about the stylistic and functional features and nuances, or the benefits of, say, an embellished Achilles patch or a lowered profile forefoot. But all shoe accouterments are secondary to the overall fit, and to that point, climbers have the same objective for the shoes they wear: to fit into the snuggest pair possible. This is done by minimizing the amount of extra space between one's crammed toes and the leather. Most climbing shoes are also designed to securely encase and maintain the subtle curvature that the average foot takes on when it is scaling a wall. The longstanding and widespread (albeit uninformed) maxim that a pair of climbing shoes should be "tight" around the foot is a little misleading, as deliberate discomfort would be a hindrance to performance rather than an enhancement of it. In a sense, the ultimate goal with any pair of climbing shoes is to have them feel like a second skin on the feet, and in that regard, they resemble ballet slippers more than athletic shoes.

Thus, it's rather amusing to survey the history of climbing footwear because unlike most other recreational footwear—tennis shoes, basketball high-tops, sneakers—they weren't born out of the Converse's Chuck Taylor All Stars template. In the shadowy light of climbing's early days, essentially any time before the 1930s, the common practice was to scale rocks in clunky boots, making no functional separation between the shoes that one wore to hike to a mountain and the shoes that one donned to actually climb it. Consider mountain climbing shoe advice in British alpinist Clinton Thomas Dent's pamphlet from the 1800s, which suggested the use of leather boots that completely covered the ankles and were soled with wrought-iron nails.

It wasn't until the 1950s and '60s that climbing shoes started deviating significantly from the heavy duty-boot model, thanks in part to tweaks that European climbers and cobblers had made in the previous decades. But footwear also began to evolve due to a changing clientele. The United States caught up to Europe's fascination with climbing and began developing its own dirtbag culture. Particularly in California, around Yosemite, the climbing scene was increasingly attracting ruffians and wandering youths who were creative and bright-eyed ne'er-do-wells.

In his account of spending years at Yosemite's now-legendary climbing nucleus, the nondescript campgrounds at Camp 4, author Steve Roper says, "Once the home of about a half-dozen climbing bums—people scorned by most tourists and nonclimbers—the campground sported 10 times that number by 1970, and rock climbing had become a respectable activity, one that increasing numbers of park visitors paid money to do."

Initially, fashion and functionality were ancillary to simply climbing and living a bare-bones existence. The climbers of Camp 4, at least in the earliest days, climbed in whatever ratty street clothes they owned, and in whatever footwear they could get their feet into—boots, raggedy sneakers, klettershoes, leather moccasins—or even just barefoot. This casualness eventually leveled out somewhat, however, and rubber-based, climbing-specific shoes became the norm.

But how pint-sized Camp 4 came to be the key cornerstone bridging the era's counterculture with the era's outdoor recreation, and eventually ushering in everything from new hardware to new shoes to new climbing styles, is now deep-seeded climbing lore. It started with something I could wholeheartedly relate to: people were simply doggedly determined to spend the summer seasons climbing.

In his book *Camp 4: Recollections of a Yosemite Rockclimber*, Roper acknowledges that the larger social panorama of the time, more so than just an urge to climb, also drove many young people in America to find trust, truth and meaning in their own pursuits: "Why did we spend so much time in the [Yosemite] Valley? Perhaps the key word is 'rebellion.' Many of us regarded the 1950s and 1960s as a time when the world—and especially our country—had lost its way. We saw materialism and complacence during the Eisenhower years. John Kennedy gave youth hope, but the events at Dallas made youth despair. An outpost called Vietnam forced its way into an unwilling national psyche. It was a hard time to be proud of our country. Perhaps we stayed close to the cliffs because we didn't want to join mainstream society. We Valley cragrats of the sixties were mostly college dropouts going no-where, fast. Intellects inhabited the campground—and so did an equal number of pseudo-intellects."

While Yosemite and other spots were blowing up in popularity in America, climbing was ratcheting up in Europe as well, and this was particularly epitomized by a Spanish climber named Miguel Gallego, who in the late 1970s got shoe manufacturer Boreal to design a light, snug-fitting shoe with a revolutionary smooth rubber outsole—as opposed to the heavily-textured and raised-heel outsole of most hiking and canyoneering boots. Known as the Firé, the shoes jolted the climbing community due to the degree at which they en-hanced footgrip on the rock and lessened the level of difficulty of many existing routes.

Pairs of Boreal Firés weren't ubiquitous in the in-ternational climbing community for a couple of years, which allowed their reputation to spread by word of mouth and swell into something of near-legend before the shoes even hit the American retail market. In the early 1980s, Gallego, with Firés in tow, traveled to Yosemite and intermingled with John Bachar, who was noted at the time for establishing solid climbing routes in Joshua Tree and Yosemite. Gallego shared information about the shoe's design with Bachar, who immediately saw the advantages of the smooth, sticky rubber outsole and its potential application on Yosemite's granite. According to the legend, Bachar ordered more than 200 pairs of Firés, with the intention of retailing them out of a little California store. Yosemite climbers lined up outside the door before the store opened, and Bachar's lot sold out almost immediately.

Whether or not the anecdote is true, it's a fact that by the mid-1980s, the Boreal Firé was the shoe of choice for climbers all over the world, and every other company quickly clamored to copy the sticky rubber design.

The essence of that design is still the industry stan-dard today, and it's remarkable how little the climbing shoe aesthetic has changed over the past 30 years.

That's not to say advancements haven't been made. For one thing, the Firés were a high top, and many sport-

A pair of vintage Boreal's Firé shoes
Photo: Courtesy of the Scottish Mountain Heritage Collection

climbing shoes nowadays allow for open ankles. But it illustrates just how groundbreaking Boreal's design was and how its template continues to prove effective. When I dug up a photo of the Firés from the 1980s, Zooey's first response wasn't that they appeared archaic, but rather, "They look really cool—I'd be happy with a pair of those."

Zooey and I took the subway to Jongno 5-ga Station, a hub in Seoul of cluttered retail shops, in search of not the Firés, which are no longer on the market but occasionally draw ogling at auctions due to their cult following. Instead, we sought something snug and budget-friendly.

We strolled along hidden side streets lined with racks of shoes for all-things outdoorsy—climbing, hiking, sailing and kayaking. It was as if a black market, a gray market, and authorized retailers had combined into a neurology of back roads and footwear vending nooks. Among the wide selection of climbing shoes, there were variations on the lacing system—some were Velcro, some were slip-on moccasins, some were tie-laces—but they all still sported the smooth, slate-black rubber bottoms and relatively minimalistic upper of the Firés of yesteryear.

Inside the retail shops, all the climbing equipment was given a designated wall, on which hung loose harnesses, chains of assorted carabiners, more shoes, windbreakers, chalk bags, athletic tape and chopsticks and other eating utensils—the latter in deference to Koreans' common practice of eating to celebrate a completed afternoon of climbing. The shops had a homey feel to their single-room interiors, many of them also sporting a corner television and a table where the employees could snack and converse with customers over coffee or tea. In fact, a few times when Zooey and I asked employees for a particular shoe style in a particular size, we felt guilty at our obvious interruption of an elaborate lunch.

All this is to say, the inside of nearly every shop smelled of a peculiar fusion of shoe leather, synthetic clothing fabric and pickled vegetables, and browsing involved an amusing wade through jumbled racks of clothes and climbing hardware in close quarters. It was in stark contrast to the massive, open-spaced retail shops of the United States, and more than once we found ourselves digging and clawing through cardboard boxes of assorted pre-owned shoes and sandals.

We finally came to a hodgepodge shop of outdoor hardware and soft goods off the main drag, on a side street of a side street. We were greeted by a college-aged employee who spoke in smooth salesmanese and told us how categorically lucky we were to have wandered into his shop. When Zooey requested a particular climbing shoe style in a particular size, our savvy saleskid told her with drooping eyebrows that the particular style was sold out across the entire Korean peninsula—a rather dubious claim, but not really something we could easily verify or disprove.

So, we took his word for it, and nodded as he suggested a different shoe style. He used a long wooden dowel to pull a shoebox down from an overhead rack. The entire tower of shoeboxes became unstable as more were withdrawn and Zooey tried on different sizes. At one point, she gritted her teeth and pressed her heel into a shoe that was too small, even by snug climbing shoe standards, and she turned to me and said, "I feel like one of Cinderella's stepsisters."

After a sizeable chunk of time, and with Zooey's feet red from multiple attempts at cramming into constrictive pairs of various models, she decided on bright red and yellow leather low-tops, size European 35, without any room in the forefoot to spare.

We thanked the young employee, who kindly offered Zooey a discount and some free athletic tape if she'd pay in cash.

We exited the shop with a pristine new pair of climbing shoes, some tape and some new hand chalk for good measure, then walked through the muggy brume of the afternoon with one thing on our minds. We slipped into the subway, and as if we were both coasting along the same polished wavelength, Zooey turned to me with her shoebox in hand and eagerly said, "Let's climb."

15 | Into the tribe

The latter part of summer accelerated. Suddenly, nights were a little cooler, the buzz of cicadas blasted through the dusk, and August days clipped by in snapshot memories of morning hikes and drinks of aloe-and-crushed-ice on my apartment deck, afternoons spent rereading David Roberts' collection of climbing essays, *Moments of Doubt*, which had served as a mainstay in my travel bag ever since I received the paperback as a gift years ago.

But in between all the mornings of climbing and the afternoons of reading, I spent some time volunteering at a youth center in Seoul that aided North Korean defectors in adjusting to democratic, big-city life. In a makeshift classroom filled with a multitude of academic and recreation teaching materials—everything from spare guitars to soccer balls and textbooks—I frequently hung out with a dozen children of varying ages and backgrounds, helped them with their school entrance essays, and did my best to answer their elaborate questions about the oddities of American pop culture (and realized in the process that my summer of climbing had resulted in hardly any awareness of new music, celebrity blather or movie releases—a refreshingly blank cultural slate that I was in no hurry to scuff up again). Inevitably, three precocious young boys who had recently arrived in South Korea posed the question to me: "What do you do in your spare time?"

I explained my preference for waking up early and getting on a nearby wall before the midday sun scorched the rocks and baked the woodlands, before everywhere was sweltering save for a few shaded, under-tree havens.

Naturally this was met with the utmost childhood bewilderment—the fact that anyone would willingly rise in the wee hours of the morning, much less do so in order to venture voluntarily into the stifling heat, seemed an act of profound absurdity and senselessness to the young boys. On top of that, considering that North Korea's school system typically doesn't teach children much about cultures of the Western world, the

A tribe of well-padded climbers at the Triple Crowne
Bouldering Competition at Rumbling Bald, NC
Photo: Mike Reardon

concept of sport climbing had understandably never been explicitly taught to the boys. But there was a stint of downtime
in the classroom later, after the youth center had provided a
lunch of rice, grilled beef and sliced lotus root for the children.
I headed outside with the same three boys to a grassy square
lined with benches, a gazebo and pull-up bars. The boys
were curious to learn more about my strange pursuit of early
morning rock climbing, and a lack of real rock in the vicini-
ty called for resourceful measures. We gathered around the
sidewall of the youth center building—old, protruding brown
brick chipped and notched in enough places to be passable as
a climbing wall, at least for demonstrative purposes.

　　I knelt at the corner base of the sidewall, nudged my
toes into shallow chipped indentations in between the jutting
bricks, pulled myself up and tried to explain the concept of
center of gravity in rudimentary terms. The boys watched
with wide eyes and even clapped as I moved my feet to
smaller indentations. Never mind the fact that I was, in the
process, literally teaching the next bored generation of youths
how to better scale the outside walls of city structures, how
to crimp on brick, and how to balance their toes on the ex-

posed drainpipe—the effects and consequences of such lessons would be anyone's guess.

But in the moment, I could read the looks on the boys' faces: they wanted to give it a try.

So, one by one, I helped the boys smear their sneakers into the bricks and pull up to a standing position, then traverse our makeshift bouldering problem across the length of the sidewall—or as far as they could get before their feet popped off or their fingertips stung from gripping the gritty bricks.

One gem from Roberts' *Moments of Doubt*: "Recently I went climbing at the Shawangunks, and found myself tiptoeing up the third pitch of a classic route called Yellow Ridge. I had climbed it once before, 20 years earlier. The moves were somehow familiar. Yet what struck me all at once was how breathtaking and bizarre climbing was." Perhaps nothing could have better captured the inexplicable—"bizarre"—aspect better than a still shot of my aiding the teenagers in their shaky-footed attempts to tiptoe and finger-pinch across the outside brick wall of a nondescript youth center. Roberts adds, "It was that there was something special about the sport, some intricacy of deed that takes hold of the spirit and asks it fundamental questions."

Roberts was reflecting on a glorious writing and mountaineering career that had spanned decades and notable climbing regions all over the world. The young boys on the outside sidewall in Seoul, on the other hand, soon raced inside the youth center to eat a dessert of fruit candy and bite-sized chocolate pies.

Still, I was left wondering about my summer obsession, the hastening of the season and a peculiar and fitting capstone to it all, a brick wall was no longer just a brick wall.

Days later, I was again discussing climbing with a community of a different sort, the regulars of Astroman Climbing Gym, on a windy evening in the tawny light of a narrow street. We ducked into a restaurant, took a seat at a low red table under curvilinear neon signage and picked at a colorful array of appetizers. Zooey was there, as was a young climbing couple—Soohang Lee and Wookyung Kim. Wookyung's ankle was swollen and bandaged from landing crookedly on it after failing to grip a leaping finisher hand-hold at the bouldering gym. He propped up his foot in front of his seat, and said that he'd be back to 100 percent in no time—that every day away from climbing made him more anxious to climb than ever before.

"You're a badass," I said to him, which prompted an amusing explanation to my Korean friends of the meaning of *badass*. And I took it as the prime opportunity to instill a wide array of climbing slang into their vocabulary, however silly and inadequate I felt imparting an up-to-date climbing vernacular: *stoked, psyched, whipped, amped, chossed, red-pointed, flashed.*

Deeper into the evening, I sat at the table, sipped a tin cup of water and watched as a table next to ours became all smiles as a waiter served them a large plate of thick shrimp. There was down-tempo music playing from corners of the restaurant, plunky electronic beats lost occasionally in our loud group conversation, all the talk revolving around climbing at first but then dispersing to a number of topics: proposed river rafting trips, cross-country hikes, dream European vacations—modest ambitions in the grandiose scheme. If climbing offers fundamental questions in its quintessence of isolation, something must be said of its communal nature as well. And one learns throughout a season of zealously pursuing anything that the true joy comes largely in being able to obsess not of something, but with someone, anyone.

We all sat around plucking rice and cabbage with our chopsticks, toasting with potent soju mixed with beer—all of the reverie enveloped in the scent of meat cooking from grated flames in the center of our table—and effectively *carpe-d* the *noctem* in the form of late-night conversation about the recent Psicobloc Masters Series climbing event in Park City, Utah. The competition had been unique because it entailed climbers racing side-by-side up identical routes 55 feet above a pool of water without the protection of ropes; the possibility of climbers falling and splashing into the blue water far below—a subcategory of climbing known as deep-water soloing—added a degree of novelty and made the whole event a little more visually exciting and spectator-friendly.

But the event was also unique in that it drew all the top stars of the sport, an unprecedented Dream Team-esque roster of professional climbers that had come together largely because everyone wanted to be involved in the event and support the concept. I couldn't help but note that our humble climbing community at the restaurant in South Korea had also come together because everyone wanted to be involved in the discussion.

It prompted me to wonder to what purpose such groups—such tribes—serve in climbing, which also has its share of isolated, individualistic demands. Dr. Stephen Schmid, a climber who teaches philosophy at the University of Wisconsin-Rock County, but more pertinently, has actually edited a book titled *Climbing — Philosophy for Everyone*, told me that the inquiry really enlarges into the greater realm of human nature. "Is our nature individualistic or communal?" he posed rhetorically. "That is a question that philosophers, psychologists, and other social scientists have tried and are still trying to answer. And, one can find arguments for the extremes and most points in between. There are some psychological theories of motivation and behavior that see relations and community as a basic psychological need, one that explains some—if not most—aspects of human behavior."

Schmid was quick to point out that the reliance on partners in climbing makes climbing akin to other team sports—and as a result, very non-individualistic. And yet, the end goal of climbing is uniquely open-ended. What does it mean to *win* at climbing? The answer is moot because the question is flawed.

To further explain the matter, Schmid referenced a landmark climbing essay from 1967 titled, "Games Climbers Play," by Lito Tejada-Flores. In the essay, Tejada-Flores asserts that climbing is better viewed more like a loose confederation of disciplines than a single sport. In that confederation, the different activities possess their own challenges and delights. Additionally, and unique when compared to other sports or recreations or lifestyle-defining pursuits, tenets and decrees of what are acceptable or unacceptable in climbing are settled on by climbers themselves—in other words, a situation of chalky-handed, rock-loving inmates running the asylum.

The guidelines that climbers informally set, unsurprisingly, are perpetuated by those climbers doing the most impressive routes; the lesser-skilled climbers who watch in wonder and amazement can't help but want to imitate the mastery. Thus, the climbing collective, all levels and measures of experience included, gives birth to a tradition.

Schmid summed up the essay and the larger issues at hand nicely: "What is interesting is that there is no governing body determining all the rules," he said to me. "The rules are whatever arises from the climbers who participate in and make up that climbing community. In essence, there arises a social contract both defining and governing various climbing communities."

When my dinner with the regulars from Astroman Climbing Gym had finished, the final chugs of beer gulped, and I wandered into the empty streets at 3:00 in the morning, I was weighing the question that ultimately had no mass, the climbing mythos as real and as elusive as ever: *individualistic or communal*? Undeniably climbing exists as a craft that is a lot of both. And with that thought, I stumbled to my apartment in the humid night and passed out on my bed, unknowingly sleeping soundly right on top a lumpy pile of my climbing harness, chalk bag and belay device.

16 | Climbing and staying grounded

A week later, I was airing out my climbing shoes, sorting some gear on my apartment deck and listening to an English-language news channel expound on the threat of nuclear annihilation on the Korean peninsula. I tossed a mess of climbing rope onto the floor, the loops winding over each other in a kaleidoscope of neon lines, and took a few moments to coil the entire heap into a tight bundle. I looked outside to a row of glassy apartment buildings across the alley and saw an elderly lady tending to her own respective chores, hanging damp linen shirts on a clothesline from her balcony high above the ground. I waved from the corner of my deck, but my greeting went unnoticed. On my TV, a newscaster was referencing a digital map of the Pacific Ocean. The grand question of the hour was: Assuming North Korea developed nuclear weapons, how far could the doomsday bombs travel? On the map, Hawaii sat like a green, exposed crumb on the vast blue blanket of the ocean—4,300 miles from North Korea, and conceivably within striking distance of a modern nuclear missile.

Of course, to someone like me sitting in an apartment in South Korea, a stone's throw from the heavily armed North Korean border, a map and precise distance calculations were not necessary; total nuclear destruction of South Korea, international news sources had asserted, could happen within a matter of milliseconds, and the entire lot of day-to-day tediums like coiling rope and drying laundry would be engulfed in a bright light of fire and 21st Century brimstone. It was more than a little disheartening, no matter how bubbly and eloquently the newscaster delivered the information.

I decided to turn off the TV, scrub the caked mud from the rubber soles of my climbing shoes with lemon juice and an old toothbrush and boil water for coffee. When my teapot whistled and rattled on the gas stove, I poured the water over a filter full of coffee grounds that had recently been mailed to me from a good friend in New York. I sipped the hot coffee on my deck and did my best to ignore the possibility that mankind's lasting accomplishment after millennia of evolution and wonder could be to press a little remote control button that would launch a few bombs and consequently obliterate everything.

I flipped through a guidebook of nearby climbing routes. I poured another mug of coffee and thought about *Columbus*, Dan's project route. Dan didn't like when I asked him questions specifically about the route, which I could understand. I knew that he had recently internalized all the moves and streamlined the mechanics into a compulsory choreography, and discussing any of it would be like talking to your baseball pitcher during a no-hitter—or at least that's how I interpreted Dan's silence on the matter. Superstition, exasperation, whatever it was, I got it.

Feeling sedentary then, likely due to seeing the names of South Korea's hundreds of climbing routes laid out in the guidebook in neat, successive lists and realizing that I'd need a lifetime of summers to get my fill of them all, I tossed my gear into my mesh bag and headed out for a climb.

I met Dan, and we drove to a crag that had numerous routes bolted at a secluded, corner wilderness. Horizontal columns of rock stood out from flatter backdrop walls like humongous chelicerae on an ancient gray face. We uncoiled the rope and traded belays up one saw-toothed corner of tall stone, then climbed a wider rock face with bulging, rhombular handholds.

At one of the crag's pointed peaks, I pulled myself over the lip and took a seat on a patch of moss to rest before climbing down. I could see the tops of the trees that receded in a uniform green cluster. The nearby hills were carpeted in earth tones too and punctuated by dark stone outcroppings.

I took a pen and scrap paper from my pocket and made a note of the way the trees and rocks in the distance looked like miniature museum pieces.

I had kept Dan updated on how my writing was progressing—he always smiled in surprise and self-consciousness when I'd tell him about a particular passage in which he appeared. He had asked me many times what exactly my

The author on a chunky route in South Korea
Photo: Dan Kojetin

book was about, as my general explanation of a summer of climbing sounded vague and unrefined. But finally, I was able to gather my thoughts into an explanation: "Many books talk about reaching the top of a specific mountain—or at least talk about trying to reach the top of a particular mountain or sending a big wall," I said, and Dan nodded at this.

"But," I said, "what about the times when you don't have a big wall or summit as an end goal, when you just want to get on the rocks as often as possible? Why are we driven to climb in those cases? I want to write about those feelings, and why those feelings never go away."

I had climbed with Dan at a number of crags, but once I saw above the trees and jotted notes about the scenery, it was as if I could feel more reasons for the pursuit beginning to solidify. Dan and I had climbed on clear days and cloudy days; Dan had wisped up technically knuckle-busting routes while I, in my eager state, had hopped on routes that felt light-years out of my league. But we continued to climb—on difficult routes or pedestrian routes, in gyms or outdoors—because the technical challenge was just one speck on the far more elaborate spectrum. It was a gamut that was part anthropological, part physiological and part *soul*ogical, at times universal and at other times entirely personal. The affinity for climbing doesn't, in fact, well up from one veiled space, although primordial predilections contribute a portion of the act. Rather, an affinity comes about as an elemental reaction to the timeless sensation of skin gripping stone, our physicality linked directly with the natural world in a sort of unbroken current. Climbing is an integral part of the continuum. The act—the vertical movement—is an ongoing story, as is its discourse. And if the rest of the world was doomed to political implosions and nuclear explosions—which I was actually less pessimistic about once I got some fresh air, a good climb, and thrust the gloom from my mind—then anyone could at least seek small moments of clarity and simplicity wherever he could find them.

Consider the case of one climber that I had learned about named William Munder. Munder had been a long-time heroin addict, and in the process, had also struggled with crack cocaine and meth addiction. At its worst, his drug abuse had resulted in failed relationships, lost jobs, wrecked personal finances and a ravaging of his mental well-being. Munder had been a self-professed junkie with a bleak future. However, in the late 1990s, he made a push to get clean with the help of Narcotics Anonymous, and it was climbing, of all activities, that would prove to be a functional supplement to the organization's recovery principles. First, Munder was intrigued by an advertisement in a local newspaper announcing the grand opening of a climbing gym near his home in Miami, Florida. Next, on a whim, he and his Narcotics Anonymous sponsor decided to give the new gym a try. What followed was an instant connection to the challenges offered by the various routes, and those challenges aided in a transformation of Munder's lifestyle. He and his sponsor began climbing several times a week, meeting other climbers and working up to harder climbs. Munder began climbing outdoors as well, and eventually he started teaching climbing to others. The physical demands of climbing, as well as the solidarity and the mentorship, helped Munder establish some self-esteem in his life at a time, shortly after quitting his drug habits, when his self-esteem had nearly bottomed out. Even after nearly 20 years of recovery, it was climbing and nature that continued to provide Munder with a foundation for life's inexhaustible twists and turns.

All that is to say, if a season outdoors teaches one anything, it's that there's just as much transcendence to be found staring up at mountains as there is standing on their summits, gazing down on the treetops, surrounded by the natural architecture of rock. Munder was a testament to that, and in a wholly different way, my own summer was as well.

When I was back in my apartment that night, I got a call from Zooey. She was taking a break from a grueling yoga-and-kettlebell workout, so I told her about the day's refreshing climb while she caught her breath over the phone.

Zooey said that she had recently returned from a family party that had been held to celebrate her nephew turning one year old. There's a Korean custom during the birthday celebration, Zooey explained, that involves placing the birthday infant in front of various representative items on a table—coinage, a paintbrush, a pen, cloth. The custom stresses that whichever item the infant gravitates toward and grasps first will indicate his passion in life—economics, the arts, politics, business. Her little nephew, in grand ambition, had chosen colorful cloth, and thus, he would grow up to be creative and industrious. Certainly nothing wrong with that. But Zooey must have known what I was thinking because she said that there was still hope that her nephew would grow up to be a climber. In a perfect dirtbag world, Zooey and I decided then and there, the table of representative items would also include a carabiner, quickdraw or compass—something to signify that sometimes the best course in life is whichever one keeps you closest to the natural world.

17 | In space and time

Dan's folks came to visit him at the tail end of August, which kept him busy and essentially took him out of climbing commission for several days. This left Zooey and me to seek out a few bouldering spots together on Jeju Island. We hipped the crash pad to a dried out riverbed punctuated by massive stones—dark gray masses set atop the sandy riverbed for as far as we were able to gaze down the contouring valley. It made for the perfect bouldering retreat, the land sunken low enough from centuries of erosion to funnel a steady breeze, and covered enough by the trees on the riverbank to remain relatively shaded in the midday heat.

But the main quirk of the dry riverbed was the fact that it was prone to flash floods, which would consequently reshuffle some of the massive boulders on a frequent basis. The result, when the floodwater evaporated and the riverbed dried out once again, was a new sequence of boulders—some rocks turned over by the water, others washed away altogether. Thus, no boulder—and no bouldering problem—were ever permanent, and new bouldering sequences were constantly being made in newfound places.

Zooey and I planted our crash pad on top of a lump of sand, at the base of a bumpy 12-foot boulder at a bend in the riverbed. The boulder was beautifully pitted, with smooth, juggy notches at the bottom and the top, to provide perfect starting and finishing handholds. We scrubbed away moss on the stone and picked dirt out of the littlest divots. We then planned out a number of problems that worked their meandering ways up different sides of the boulder, the highlight being a nine move crimp-haul up an inclined section of the rock. Zooey named the bouldering problem *Koala Bear*, on account of the way one had to unabashedly hug an upper portion of the boulder at the crux.

It was around our sixth or seventh attempt on *Koala*

Bear that we noticed the frogs. There were a bunch of them—more frogs, in fact, than I had ever seen in a single place. They were orange-bellied and roughly the size of a nickel, swimming and hopping in nearby puddles in the sand. In between bouldering sessions, Zooey and I stayed entertained by watching the smallest frogs of the bunch venture out of their respective puddles, brave the vast expanse of sand and maneuver in between the larger stones to find another puddle. We were left to wonder why the frogs left their puddles in the first place, into the enormous unknown for the sake of simply making the journey.

Zooey Ahn focused and crimped on a boulder problem
Photo: Zooey Ahn

By the time the afternoon lost its bright hue, Zooey and I were exhausted from bouldering. Our fingers were ragged. We reclined on the crash pad, among the frog-filled puddles. I played a harmonica while Zooey dozed off. A patch of clouds seemed to unfold above us and fill the sky with thick, white tufts. The steady breeze continued to crawl through the river valley.

It was then that it hit me swiftly and surprisingly— this was it, the end of summer. The months and weeks that had seemed infinitely laid out in a lovely line in front of me had somehow come and gone. Even the final days of August, which I had clung to in security as my last vestiges of blistering summer warmth and free time, had glided by in a great arc. The previous week, Zooey and I had been climbing near Seoul, and now we were in the scattered boulders of the Jeju riverbed, relaxing in the thin lines of light shining through breaks in the trees, soaking in the dreamy, hyper-end of the season.

I gazed around at the rocks and the shadows coming off of the sheer stone embankments. There was no other person in sight except for Zooey, and we enjoyed the quiet area for a long while before cleaning up, changing out of our climbing shoes and packing up our gear. We said a goodbye to the *Koala Bear* boulder—climbers have a tendency to develop a strange kinship with a specific route or problem. But this goodbye felt particularly melancholy, not because the boulder was full of phenomenal sequences by any means, but because of its delicate place in space and time. Soon the fall typhoons would come, and nearly everything in the river bend would be washed downstream. Many of the boulders would be resettled and resequenced, or covered by sand and smaller rocks altogether. Then out of the disarray from the storms and floods, the boulders would eventually settle. The sand would dry again, and new starting handholds and footholds would be found in the immense rocks. New bouldering problems would be established on seemingly new, river-washed stones, all residing in some other position or place yet to be known—a place that Zooey and I might never find.

18 | Following the routes of our heroes

Fall semester began at the university and I eagerly accepted my teaching duties. The Korean campus that had been like a ghost town for an ample chunk of the summer started to buzz with conversation. Benches and blankets under the early fall sunshine were now occupied with bookbag-toting 20-somethings, and busier still were the nights when the tennis and basketball courts held matches and scrimmages under the tall lights of the outdoor stadium. In one fell swoop, the university grounds suddenly became a hub of academic kinetic energy.

In one of my classes, I taught Ralph Waldo Emerson's famous essay, "Uses of Great Men," to a couple dozen students still perpetually groggy from summer's end. My mind as well, if I would pause and reflect under the shady pines along the campus sidewalks, was still anchored by the past summer's climbing indulgences.

"All mythology opens with demigods, and the circumstance is high and poetic; that is, their genius is paramount," Emerson says in the essay. I couldn't help but recall the mythos of climbing that I first knew long ago. I remembered seeing a photograph of free-solo luminary Dan Osman hanging off the side of a beige slab without ropes or a harness, his legs splayed out from the rock in total freedom. As a young climber myself, that picture had epitomized the courageous boundaries of the sport. However, thinking back on the image as an adult, I saw it more as epitomizing something broader and grander, the existential limits of mankind—Osman dangling precariously between tiny rock handholds and the eternity that awaited him if he let go. "Nature seems to exist for the excellent," Emerson says. "The world is upheld by the veracity of good men; they make the earth wholesome."

I recalled, as well, my admiration for Jim Holloway, one of America's first great boulderers. According to legend,

Holloway would take weeks to create a single bouldering problem in the western United States. In the process of such systematic design, he took the meticulous aspects of setting bouldering problems or climbing routes to new levels. Holloway was quite a different character than Dan Osman, but both were equally devoted to the extraordinary and disciplined conception of human movement on stone.

It is safe to say, then, that a survey of the great men and women of the climbing craft becomes more a study of obsession, of becoming so engrossed and engaged and infatuated with the rocks and the entire vertical process that nothing else matters. For a prime example of this, one need not look any further than Alex Honnold, who famously lived in a van for years, eschewing the comforts of a conventional home life in order to travel the country, live on the road and essentially climb on a full-time basis. Countless dirtbags throughout history have adopted a similar peripatetic lifestyle, enjoying a beautiful, frugal trajectory around the world's diverse crags and mountains, the act of climbing serving always as the nucleus.

During my own summer of continually crimping fingertips into stone cracks and edging the tips of my shoes onto the smallest rock nubs, I felt climbing as an inherent eagerness to take in things from new angles, my eyes constantly scanning the walls for another route or another bouldering problem. It was, for me, a way of taking in various challenges by degrees, and separating them by extraordinary moments.

I kept my climbing harness and climbing shoes stored in the desk drawer of my university office, just in case I was ever presented with the sudden chance to steal away for a quick pitch up a wall somewhere, anywhere. But it was wishful thinking on my part, as my days quickly filled with student advising sessions and literature lessons to plan, more essays to discuss, papers to grade and meetings to attend. I was left to miss being on the wall, under the heavy heat of summer or amid the intermittent post-monsoon mist, to a point where it became a feeling of longing once again. I craved the walls, which is to say that summer climbing hadn't been a whim, but a pursuit far more compound and intricate—and primal.

Dan and I met at 9:00 one evening. It was too dark to climb outside anywhere, but I grabbed my shoes and chalk bag and we drove to a dilapidated, single-room climbing gym. Dan had joined the gym's climbing club, and as a result, we had been given a key to the facility and granted 24-hour access. We entered and swatted away a cloud of mosquitoes in the dim light, then switched on a few old, metallic fans to get some air flowing through the stuffy space. We talked about our recent ambitions of founding a climbing club at the university. "I'd ultimately like to teach climbing," Dan said while we rested on dusty bouldering mats after warming up. "But I don't know how I'd teach it. I don't know why I do certain moves, or how to explain the mechanics."

I thought about his statement for a moment. Finally, I said, "I guess you just get people on the walls first, and everything else will happen from there."

We worked our way around the walls of the room, traversing a couple of long endurance routes, never more than a few inches off the ground, never pushing the pace or getting too pumped. But still, I felt exalted to be climbing, to be feeling the strain in my shoulders and forearms, tightening my grip on well-worn holds in a ramshackle indoor gym. An entire obsessive summer in the books and I still hadn't had enough. I still wasn't ready to relegate climbing to some lesser space, a space less than requisite and necessary.

On the drive home, Dan told me that he'd made a decision to leave South Korea at the end of the semester. His graduate work would be finished then, his thesis would be approved, and he'd be free to go anywhere in the world. He hadn't decided yet where he'd go next, and the fact that his girlfriend lived in South Korea would complicate the logistics of his decision. But after years in the same place, Dan was itching for a new adventure—new challenges in a new, unfamiliar space. "Maybe I'll go to France," he said to me. "I've always wanted to live in Chamonix or Fontainebleau, basically the climbing capitals of the world. It's been my dream to live and climb there for a long time."

A mandolin was strumming a bluegrass tune on a CD in Dan's car radio. We wound on a sloping road under a full-moon sky.

"It's exciting," I said. "You can do anything in any country with your graduate school degree. Every place needs conservation work."

"You're right," Dan said. "I can go anywhere, but it's almost like I don't even know where to start."

"You just go," I said. "The starting point is packing your harness and chalk bag. The rest tends to work itself out."

The mandolin tune on the radio had ended, and now a band was singing a verse from the traditional song "Shenandoah" through the car speakers, warm and folksy.

"Yeah," Dan said. "I guess if I don't like a new place, I can always go somewhere else, right?"

"Exactly," I said.

Indoors or outdoors, the challenges, mechanics and rewards of climbing are largely the same
Photo: Nejron Photo

19 | The need to compete

One of the noteworthy transmutations of the climbing craft has been its relatively recent solidification as a viable competitive sport, complete with structured competitions, world records, on- and off-seasons, World Cup tournaments, testing for performance enhancing drugs, lucrative sponsorships and all of the politics that come with turning a fringe activity into a money-making spectacle. Climbing, of course, has long possessed aspects of one-upmanship—the early days of European alpine clubs jostling for the first ascents of summits is evidence of that. But the more contemporary rise of sport-style competitions, on artificial walls all over the world, has prompted progressive motivations from the climbers themselves. Chiefly, there exists a considerable amount of "gym rats" nowadays who take to climbing because they like athletically competing—or more specifically, because they want to win. And since the founding of climbing's main, global governing body, The International Federation of Sport Climbing, in 2007, competitive ambitions don't have to be unrealistic pipe dreams for youngsters with a hankering for trophies rather than ascents.

One article in Boulder, Colorado's *Daily Camera* newspaper, written by climber and journalist Chris Weidner, asks whether climbing outside might ultimately become irrelevant for a future demographic of climbers, further emphasizing the growing audience of the indoor discipline. Weidner even notes that an appearance by climbing in an upcoming Olympics isn't out of the question, which is an idea that has been discussed for years.

When it came to gaining some perspective on all of climbing's modern, competitive expansion, there was nobody more qualified to talk to than Udo Neumann. The manager of Germany's national bouldering team and, as such, an instructor for some of the best competitive boulderers of all time like Jan Hojer and Juliane Wurm, Neumann had not only witnessed the steady influx of worldwide competitions but indirectly played a role in perpetuating the incursion.

Born in Cologne, Germany, in 1963, Neumann was intrigued by climbing magazines in the 1970s but devoted his time and competitive energy to other sports—running and then whitewater kayaking. ("An unstable environment like whitewater kayak racing was quite different from the static, controlled climbing of that time," he told me when I reached out to him late in the summer for a little insight into his personal climbing past. "I learned a lot about crisis management and the fine line between control and losing control—which is very helpful for modern bouldering.")

Neumann started climbing seriously at age 19, honing his skills on stone buildings in Europe and natural crags wherever he could. Then, in 1984, he met American climber Dale Goddard and was mesmerized by the meticulousness of Goddard's training. Neumann had formally studied sports science in school, and the climbing partnership with Goddard furthered a deep interest in the methodical subtleties of climbing-specific training.

Together, Neumann and Goddard authored *Performance Rock Climbing* in 1993—a milestone of a book that packaged climbing as a full-body, full-time, full-devotion athletic pursuit. *Performance Rock Climbing* treated climbing training as sports training, which sounds obvious now but was quite innovative and forward-thinking for the time. The book also happened to have been written and published during a period when the concept of officiated sport climbing contests was starting to gain ground—first in Europe and then in the United States.

Neumann would continue writing in the following decades, as well as working in photography and filmmaking, firmly entrenching himself in the craft's development and publicity with each endeavor. But he was, and still is, an intriguing figure in competitive climbing, as he seems to have lived two diametrically opposed climbing lives. On the one hand, *Performance Rock Climbing* played a big role in boosting climbing's status into a more formally athletic and competitive realm. With chapters like "Perceptual Approaches to Psychological Control," "Scheduling and Periodization" and "Technique Training: Theory," the book helped produce a new generation of climbers who didn't just *climb*—they trained, they practiced, they drilled. And Neumann, himself, had won several regional climbing competitions in Europe in the late-1980s, which added to the book's credibility.

On the other hand, however, Neumann had also been the epitome of a dirtbag in his 20s, freely traveling the world, climbing and living fast in places like Yosemite, Mexico, France and Iceland. He would, in fact, land an eventual job as a coach of the German climbing team, but only after he dared to veer outside of the established athletic system.

He explained to me, "In 2001, an interview with me attacking the German Alpine Club was published in the German magazine *Klettern*. The magazine interview caused quite a stir since I criticized lead competitions, route setting in lead competitions and the lame sports program of the German Alpine Club. The result was that I was considered controversial from that point on. In 2007, I started organizing international bouldering competitions with my own little format that worked quite well, and for whatever reason, in 2009, the German Alpine Club decided to try me out as a coach. After many power struggles, I implemented some helpful strategies for the bouldering team that led to success."

It was fitting, and a small thrill, to interview Neumann for my research on why we climb, as he had been affectionately deemed everything from climbing's mad scientist to a guru over the years. His views of training as a multifaceted activity that should embrace physical, mental and numinous qualities of each individual climber as needed, reflected the many components of climbing, in general.

But I was specifically curious about the competitive allure.

"The mixture of mental and physical aspects in rock climbing competition is quite unique," he said. "The problem-solving part of climbing, combined with the physical difficulty of applying force to the wall, and the fact that all of this happens slowly enough that we are aware of it, creates an interesting experience—also for the spectators. And the phenomenon that competitors inspect the problems together [before climbing them individually] is downright fascinating. There is so much interesting human interaction going on at a climbing competition—the coaches, the physics, the competitors— all in a heightened, hyper-alert state of mind during finals."

I quickly got a sense of just how serious and scientific Neumann was when approaching climbing's physicality, and how much of a coach he really was. He typically referred to his climbers as "athletes" and casually referenced intricacies that many climbers would never consider—training phases, the constant management of momentum, leg strength. Yet, he also expounded on having to handle the flipside of competition training: potential burnout of his athletes. Simply, those athletes who climb in order to win also risk pushing themselves beyond the ledge of enjoyment.

Udo Neumann, one of the pioneers of applying modern athletic training principles to climbing, is now actively involved in various forms of climbing media
Photo: Eddie Fowke

"You have to keep the stimuli fresh during the preparation phase," he said, explaining the importance of keeping training varied with his German team. "We see ourselves like Shaolin Kung fu artists, and we are always trying to improve. It's a very tiring lifestyle during the competition season, and we all need some time to come down. That's a very personal thing. Jan Hojer, for example, plays a lot of basketball in his off-time and almost doesn't climb at all, whereas Julian Wurm does a lot of other activities too, but can never keep her fingers from climbing for more than two days."

Straddling that hypothetical mental line—engaged enough to perform optimally, but not overwhelmed—is what makes bouldering competitions particularly unique and taxing in Neumann's opinion, with the constant starting and stopping inherent in short, intense bouldering sequences: "Part of the challenge of bouldering competitions is that you are constantly dragged out of that *zone*. In lead climbing, you climb for at least a couple of minutes, so you can enjoy the flow. But in bouldering, it's a constant up and down emotionally."

Still, in Neumann's opinion, there is a universal competitive quality to climbing that appears in all sports. "From Cologne, where I live, it's not too far to Fontainebleau," he said. "The bouldering there is so varied that the conception of what climbing is, and what climb moves are, tends to be broader than, say, the conception belonging to a limestone sport climber. What my athletes train is basically an extension of the complete bouldering experience with unstable elements thrown in for important mental aspects. In our team trainings, our strongest boulders tend to be the strongest in all exercises, regardless of how detached those exercises seem from climbing. Jan Hojer and Juliane Wurm, for example, are very complete athletes and would do well in many activities."

Neumann noted that while that universal competitive drive is partly nature-based and partly nurture-based, it isn't really something that can be explicitly taught. Considerably for climbing, the challenge for an athlete comes not in being able to amplify the competitive drive under the bright lights and camera flashes of a contest, but being able to mute it and, instead, relax—to slip into that flow experience.

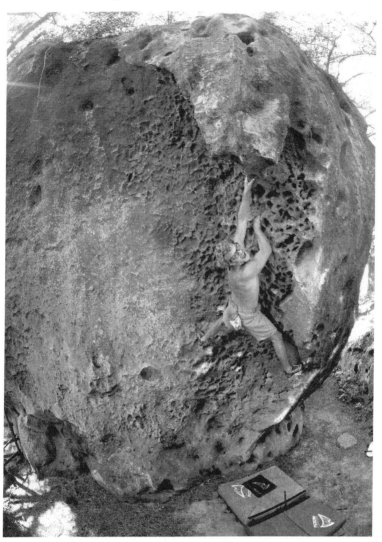

Neumann finding time to climb amid his busy schedule
Photo: Udo Neumann

At this point in the interview, I was surprised that Neumann had mentioned hardly anything about training his athletes to actually *beat* their competitors—wasn't that the groundwork upon which competitive climbing stood?

But he explained that the motivation for competitive climbers was broader. There exist so many dualities—getting to the top of a route while also beating an opponent is one such duality—that make competitive climbing truly a unique sport.

"Definitely the desire to top-out a problem comes first," he said. "Another strong motivation is the hope to show what you are capable of. Even if you don't top-out, you still can show a good performance and be happy with it. Your competitors will acknowledge that too, and the internal hierarchy is defined by that."

So, even in competition with others, climbers are driven first by those base, self-residing forces. It seemed a suitable way to bring the interview with Neumann back to my original curiosity about mankind's reasons for climbing.

It is also worth mentioning that Neumann considered climbing to be mankind's "primal locomotion," which was something he had also researched and witnessed first-hand. "In 2011, I went to Sumatra to see orangutans in the wild," he told me. "I learned so much from how the mother orangutans teach their kids to climb, how they spot them, how they create little challenges for them—they really are the best climbing coaches. And that is where we come from."

20 | Earth witness

It was the arrival of a particular Korean national holiday, the ceremonial equivalent of America's Thanksgiving, that allowed Dan, Zooey and me the free time to meet up and climb together once again. With the rest of the country subdued from feasting on enormous meals, and most businesses and restaurants operating on truncated hours, we opted to pack a lunch and take to the crags early for all-day, uninterrupted climbing.

The morning was spent on a handful of moderate routes in a dried-out riverbed. We climbed beneath low gray clouds that matched the color of the rocky embankment surrounding us. We then hiked through ferns and crept around thorny branches to find one remarkable route—an L-shaped line up a flat stone face that Dan said he'd climbed dozens of times over the years. Zooey and I both gave it a go, ground out the cruxes slowly, before Dan blazed up it effortlessly.

When Dan was back on level ground, he turned to me and said that he felt surprisingly good: "Maybe I'll even give *Columbus* a try," he said. "What do you think?"

"I think that's a perfect plan," I said. I hadn't expected Dan to get on his project route that day. In fact, I had tried to forget about *Columbus* altogether after Dan had assured me a while ago that he wasn't necessarily itching to conquer the route after all. "It's just a route," he had said nonchalantly.

But I could tell that by forcibly not allowing himself to have any expectations of success on the route, he had inadvertently created a tranquil acceptance of the route as a long-term presence in his life—regardless of whether he cared to send it or not. So, we took an hour for a lunch break, and then drove to *Columbus*, which was hidden in an expanse of woodlands, at the end of a long series of old, stone steps.

Columbus from a distance was not grotesque. It was a single pitch that curved in a steady arc to a nice finishing spot on dark orange rock. But when one got closer, it was obvious

127

that the angles of the route were unforgiving. The route began inside a cave, and the crux occurred right when the back rock started curving to create the roof of the cave; climbing *Columbus* essentially meant climbing out of the roof of the cave and continuing up a line with lousy feet and large, loose rocks.

By the time Dan was at the base of the route, a few other young climbers had gathered, taking an afternoon break from the Korean Thanksgiving festivities with their families to watch his attempt.

Dan powered through the first few bolts, and he clipped in the quickdraws to shouts of encouragement from the kids below him. He paused, shook out his arms one-by-one, and smiled—clearly feeling good about the movement up the route so far.

Dan Kojetin making steady progress on Columbus
Photo: John Burgman

High on *Columbus,* Dan pinched a sliver of a hold, swung his hips, and pulled his torso closer to the wall. The route was now revealing its full, merciless curvature.

Dan pulled on the hold a little more and moved further up the route.

I felt a wave of excitement, like an electric energy through my limbs, at the realization that Dan was going to send his long-term project.

Then, suddenly, I saw a swift blur of denim from Dan's climbing jeans. His feet had popped off their footholds right before he could clip into the fourth bolt, and his legs swung into the open air like loose pennants. I had him on belay, and I felt his weight immediately sink into the rope and tighten the entire line.

I could tell that Dan was frustrated and disappointed when his loss of footing resulted in a subsequent loss of handgrip on the rock. In an instant, his whole body peeled completely off the wall and he was left dangling from the rope.

"I really shouldn't have fallen there," he chided himself, still hanging on the rope in mid-air, the opening of the cave behind him like an enormous, dark mouth. I was about to lower him, but he said that he wanted to at least practice the sequence of moves while he was hanging up there.

He swung back to the wall, grasped the rock with his hands, secured his feet and lunged into the next move. A plume of chalk dust scattered as his fingertips latched onto the faraway handhold. He clipped his quickdraw into the fourth bolt and then briefly held a kneebar before again popping off the rock and dangling mid-air.

He cursed in frustration, which drew wide eyes and gasps from the kids gathered around the base of the route on the ground. At this, Dan laughed and quickly apologized. "Cover your ears, cover your ears," he yelled down to the kids with a grin.

The laughter lightened the mood, sloughed off some of the intensity, and rather than being lowered down, Dan again chose to stay on the route and give the movements another try.

He finally secured the kneebar and continued through the last few moves to complete the entire route.

When Dan finished and I lowered him, I expected him to be disappointed; he had wanted to send the route in a single, fluid attempt, and instead he had failed—peeled off and fallen in spots that were well within his skill level. But surprisingly, he looked up from his harness as he untied the bowline knot in the rope smiled. "That's what I call a good day," he said.

I tried to gauge if he was being genuine with his positivity or merely being sarcastic.

But he was serious, and his enthusiasm was evident as he nodded his head and shook out his arms. "At least now I really know I can do it," he said, "and that's what I'm stoked about. It's just a matter of putting it all together, but that will come someday."

We left the crag when we started to lose daylight, and I, too, felt fully content with the day and excited about Dan's optimism. *Columbus* would remain for Dan to send some other time, some other cool afternoon, and the act of making it up the route was ultimately insignificant. Covering vertical distance had very little to do with Dan's vertical aspirations, he assured me. And I felt entirely the same sentiment.

I asked Dan if he'd drop me off at the curved edge of my apartment's parking lot. I shouldered my gear and walked down a gently sloping street, then emerged at a concrete rotary edged with a gimbap restaurant, Internet café and a series of convenience stores. Hidden behind an arboretum of thin-trunked trees was a sleepy coffee shop. I stopped in to order some ginseng tea. The sharp heat radiating through the cardboard tea cup felt revitalizing against my tired, sore hands, long ago callused at the pads and fingertips.

I took my drink out the back door, to an open concrete space that was perched slightly above long yellow fields. Stalks of bamboo swayed steadily in the breeze and receded into thicker clusters of persimmon trees and not-quite-ripe tangerine canopies along the field's edge. A few straw-hatted farmers hunched in the low light, working their hands through the golden leaves and sea of dirt in silence. The end of my climbing summer—I mean the true, unabashed end of summer that is undeniable when the first ember flourishes of fall colors can be seen in the smooth treetops—came not on the top of a climbing wall or a nose's length away from polished stone. Rather, the season and all its questions and wordless, physical, mental, competitive and even spiritual dialogues with the rocks felt concluded right there, from a gaping horizontal distance.

In *The Boulder*, Francis Sanzaro writes, "One begins on the ground—the ground is not the ground, however. It is a principle of movement. Off the ground is where the battle begins, but it is also where it ends."

That statement and its cryptic implications remain among my favorite sentiments when a chapter of the climbing life closes, only to reveal new endeavors, new crags somewhere else with fresh possibilities and deeper searches within oneself. In the same book, while explaining bouldering as an independent art form, Sanzaro asks, "What exactly is our creativity? This is the first question we need to ask seriously in order to discuss our sport."

But I would argue that it is also the final question, for the many physical and cognitive processes inherent in any climb, easy or difficult, indoors or outdoors, serve the purpose of creating a bond with the chosen course—the route itself, and the rock or gym wall, and each individual hand- and foothold. Explicitly defining creativity might be a rhetorical inquiry, but there is no doubt that a climb, through its internal and external demands, can capture a moment in time and articulate emotions as audaciously and eloquently as any other art form. Like many climbers before me, I was lucky enough to have an entire season of such captured moments, which felt as validating as any possible answer to the question: Why do we climb? Asking the supreme question was an answer in and of itself, it just took a summer to let it unfurl.

I was reminded at that moment of a statue I had seen commonly in Asia, in which the Buddha sits serenely with one hand resting on his lap and the fingers of his other hand gently touching the ground. Sometimes called the Earth Witness pose, this image of the Buddha has been used for centuries to represent not only mankind's deep connection to the geographic world, but also that mankind is merely a conscious conduit in the bond of all-things physical to all-things spiritual. As the myth associated with the Earth Witness pose goes, the unenlightened Siddhartha Gautama was meditating beneath his Bodhi tree and suddenly overcome by evil forces in the form of temptation—known as Mara in Buddhist teachings—that attempted to break his concentration. The Siddhartha did not waver from his calm, meditative state, however, and when Mara asked what gives anyone the right to seek enlightenment, Siddhartha simply reached down and touched the ground. It was with this modest gesture that Siddhartha gained enlightenment and became the Buddha. The fact that the Buddha was touching dirt, rather than a rock wall, is irrelevant to the thematic meaning of the motion. By touching part of the earth, the Buddha was acknowledging that there is nothing beyond a single moment, and the given world that resides within that moment. Enlightenment doesn't come from material gain—seeking goods or services in the unpredictable future—nor does it come from focusing on the past, nor does it miraculously get bestowed upon us from someone else. Enlightenment comes purely from us, in the present and actively connected to this earth, and the earth is the observer of that veritable wakefulness.

I sipped my steaming tea and stared at the farmers, hunched in the translucent glow of the setting sun. With no oversized rocks nearby, no enormous boulders and no great stone slabs to put the scene into scale, the devoted farmers looked misplaced in the wide-open land. Their motions, adept scooping of dirt and examination of the leaves, had a ghostly grace, but it was as if some greater presence was missing from the composition; my mind desired rocks in order to construe a grander meaning. Soon it became even darker, and it was difficult to make out the hand motions of the farmers or to separate the pines from the bamboo shoots in the distance. It became difficult, too, to visually separate any of the immediate earth from the silhouetted stone that rose up far beyond the fields. It was as if the ground and the rocks and the trees and the blotted sky were in elemental uniformity—they were all together, and only together could they ever be understood or undertaken.

At home a bit later, I draped my jacket and my gear bag over a chair on the deck to air out. Through the window screens, I couldn't see much—it was just a thick black swathe of the night. But the crickets were loud, and a chilly breeze was blowing and hinting at the new season. I looked up in the direction of the sky and saw a few pixels of stars gleaming in the inkbottle atmosphere. I could sense that somewhere beyond the black mantle, in ten thousand horizons, mountains and walls existed unseeable yet ever-present in their ancient enormity.

I placed my harness and shoes and chalkbag on a shelf in my closet on the porch and I shut the door. I didn't know when I'd get the chance to climb again as often and as freely as I had in the past several months. But I also had a feeling that I would never be off the rocks for long.

Epilogue

As I was putting the finishing touches on the manuscript that would eventually become this book, I learned that several of my students at the university were interested in forming a creative writing club—a periodic meeting outside of classes during which I could help them craft fiction pieces, poems or essays, as well as offer editing tips and recommend good books about subjects that excited them. At this point, the weather had grown much chillier and rainier. Additionally, I had moved into a new apartment, so the rhythms of my life felt quite different than they had in the July or August peak of my climbing, despite the fact that summer hadn't been that long ago. I was still climbing at least three times a week, either at a local bouldering gym or outdoors on the banks of the dried-out riverbed. Climbing was still essential to me, it had just become more of a challenge to accommodate the interest as I began to take on more job responsibilities at the university.

To the delight of students, the creative writing club took off, and soon it seemed like many of them wanted to write more about the natural world. I have always particularly enjoyed literary pieces that explore the wilderness as much as they record man's place in it; paperbacks by Henry David Thoreau, John Muir, Roderick Frazier Nash and Edward Abbey were long-time staples in my Duluth pack when I'd go camping, canoeing or head deep into the woods during my youth. I was naturally eager to share those same authors with my students.

Ultimately, however, I can't take any credit for my students' interest in nature writing. Their curiosity, I think, happened entirely outside of my influence and was due to a greater awareness of the immediate environment once they started thinking like writers, like documentarians of narratives. The university campus on which they lived and attended classes was particularly wild—surrounded by hills that rose up into clouds of mist, lush forests that were filled with pines and ferns and bright wildflowers, craters that had been formed by lava millennia ago, the temperamental ocean and its tides. And all of the nature was frequently in the grip of powerful wind gusts and rainstorms. In essence, there was plenty of stimuli around them about which to write.

As a natural progression from wanting to write about the nature, the students soon expressed a desire to further explore the wild land around them. So, our creative writing club would occasionally meet, when the weather permitted, outside beneath the trees, on grassy outcroppings or smooth-rock hillsides. Even in the chillier weather, we would write and talk and share pieces of writing that had recently moved us. I read passages about climbing from various authors to them, but I also read passages about other pursuits. I have always enjoyed Sigurd Olson's musings on canoeing, and at times such writing seemed appropriate given how close we were to water.

Around the same time as all of this, I heard unexpectedly from a very dear friend from long ago. It was a correspondence that lifted my spirits. And my friend, a writer, sent me part of a poem titled, "Pipistrelles," from a book, *Song*, by Brigit Pegeen Kelly:

But we are not birds. All that is birdlike
In us, in the bats, is illusion.
There is nothing at all of the bird in us....
Except for flight. Except for flight.

I couldn't help but put the lines into a climbing context. Another section of the poem contains the following lines:

From rocks and trees, from the emptiness
We cannot resist casting into,
Is colored by the distortions of our hearts,
And what we hear almost always blinds us.
We stumble against phantoms, throw
Ourselves from imaginary cliffs, and at dusk, like children,we
Run the long shadows down.

I read the poem many times over the course of a couple weeks and thought about all that holds us, all humans, to the ground. There are such physical and conventional forces that maintain that we stay constantly and firmly to this earth. Yet, excluding the physics of our existence, there remains an inherent drive—an inquisitiveness or defiance—in so many of us, and possibly deep inside everyone, that makes us forever curious about the vertical.

It's that small compulsion that remains enough to combat all the standard practices and conventions and actually get us off the ground, moving upward.

At one of the meetings of the creative writing club, I happened to gather the students unintentionally at the base of a long rock wall on campus that would be, I realized, quite good for climbing. I took a moment to size up the stones. I noted to myself which series of holds would be chaotic and which grooves would be secure if I were to actually hop on the wall at some point and create some bouldering problems or a long traverse.

"You rock climb a lot, right?" one of the students asked me when she noticed me looking attentively at the wall, absorbed in a natural line of possible holds that I had found. The student was a runner, an avid marathoner, in fact, and she was in the midst of a grueling training regime for an upcoming 10-kilometer race. But she had never done much in the rugged outdoors, in terms of sports or exercise.

"I do," I said. "Climbing is what I love."

She then wondered out loud if our creative writing club might be able to one day do something active at the natural spots where we were so accustomed to meeting. Climbing. Hiking. Boating. "Anything outdoors," she said. "It would be an exciting way to get inspired for writing."

"I agree," I said. "Maybe we could all get on some climbing routes someday."

"I hope so," she said. "You know, rock climbing is just one of those things—I don't know why, but I've always wanted to try it."

Dan and the author at the base of a Korean crag
Photo: John Burgman

Appendix

Glossary

Belay: A safety procedure in which one individual (the belayer) uses various devices and techniques to manage the tautness and slack of the climbing rope, thereby being responsible for the security of another individual (the climber).

Bolt: A small piece of metal that is inserted into rock to act as one of the protection points, potentially holding the weight of a roped-up climber. While often not permanent, bolts typically stay in the stone for many years.

Bouldering: A discipline of rock climbing in which a rope is not used. Bouldering usually entails remaining closer to the ground than one would on a roped-up climb—although there are exceptions. Climbing particularly high while bouldering is known as *high balling*.

Carabiner: An ovular (or similarly shaped) metallic ring used to secure a climber to other equipment or modes of protection.

Chalk bag: A small pouch, often attached to a waist belt or directly to the climber's harness, which holds powdered chalk (magnesium carbonate). The chalk improves a climber's grip on the wall or rock by reducing hand sweat.

Crash pad: A rectangular, cushioned mat placed on the ground near a particular climb. The crash pad serves as a means of softening a fall and protecting a climber from injury while bouldering.

Crimping: A style of gripping that is used on slender handholds—crimp holds—that lack a substantial positive surface. The climber's fingers are curled, as if to make a partial fist, so that only the pads of the fingertips are used to secure the thin handhold.

Crux: The section of a climbing route or bouldering problem that is the most challenging. The crux can be a single movement, or it can be a longer sequence of several movements.

Dirtbag: An affectionate term for someone who is wholly devoted to a specific outdoors activity.

Dynamic movement: Climbing moves to subsequent hand- or footholds in which secure contact is made with the hold as a result of thrust and momentum, often by lunging or jumping. The opposite of *static movement.*

Dyno: Abbreviated term for a single dynamic movement, which implies lunging or leaping for a faraway handhold. John Gill was the first person to adapt the movement to climbing, calling it a "free aerial."

Free climbing: A broad category of rock climbing in which additional equipment such as ropes can be used for safety purposes but cannot be used to aid in progress of movement on the wall or rock.

Free soloing: A discipline of rock climbing in which the climber is high off the ground and without a rope. Thus, the consequences of a fall while free soloing are likely severe.

Gimbap: A common Korean snack—rice, vegetables and various other ingredients rolled up in dried seaweed.

International Federation of Sport Climbing: Based in Italy and often abbreviated as the IFSC, this is the organization that oversees climbing competition on a global scale.

Jug: (adj: *juggy*) A handhold that is large and exceptionally graspable, often due to a deep indentation or ample pocket for one's fingers.

Mountaineering: A broad label for a person's movement on a mountain, which can include technical elements of rock climbing combined with hiking, the negotiation of ice and snow and occasionally altitude acclimation.

The Nose: One of the oldest and most popular climbing routes on El Capitan in California's Yosemite National Park.

Problem: In bouldering, the problem is the collective, designated hand- and foot-hold sequences of a given climb. In other climbing disciplines, the sequence required to climb the rock is called the route.

Quickdraw: Two carabineers linked together with dog bone-shaped webbing—or some variation of such design—that is used to attach a climber's rope to safety protection on the wall.

Send: To successfully climb all of a route, either by reaching the top or by reaching the route's designated end.

Soju: A Korean alcoholic beverage typically gulped from a shot glass or mixed with beer.

Sport climbing: A discipline of rock climbing in which the route is usually pre-determined and bolts have already been placed in the rock or wall—or an anchor has already been placed at the top of the route—to protect the climber in the case of a fall.

Static movement: Climbing moves to subsequent hand- or foot-holds in which secure contact is made with the hold first, followed by the steady transfer of weight or necessary shift in one's center of gravity. The opposite of *dynamic movement*.

Trad climbing: Abbreviated term for traditional climbing. A discipline of rock climbing in which the rock does not include pre-placed bolts. Rather, the climber carries various forms of protection on his person and places them as needed into the rock.

Zen: A particular discipline of Buddhism. While complex in theory, the essence of Zen is ultimate simplicity in the ultimate present, often sought through a meditative act or calm observation.

A note on grades

For those who might be unfamiliar with how rock climbs are systematically assessed: There is no universal system for grading a climb's difficulty or severity. Rating systems vary depending on the country or region in which the climb exists, and even then, there is wide variation depending on who graded the route. A myriad of factors can contribute to a route's general difficulty, including the incline of the wall or rock face, the sizes and shapes of the holds for one's hands and feet, the intricacy of the required movements, and the distance between the holds.

In this book, on the occasion that grades were mentioned, I mostly referenced the Yosemite Decimal System. It is the grading system that is widely used in the United States, and it is also a grading system that is widely accepted in South Korea. Under the Yosemite Decimal System, a route is typically graded according to the most difficult single move of the entire move set. Most standard rock climbs under the Yosemite Decimal System begin with a 5 and are then followed by a decimal that denotes the more technical degree of difficulty. A climb that is rated 5.10, for example, is easier than a climb that is rated 5.12. Alphabetical tags might be given to further designate a climb's technical complexity: 5.12a, 5.12b, 5:12c, 5:12d.

Bouldering has similarly varied systems for grading difficulty. Much of the United States and South Korea use the V-scale, which is also sometimes called the Hueco Rating System. Increasing integers are given to designate the increasing difficulty of a bouldering problem: V4, V5, V6, V7, etc.

There's a lot of nuance that goes into grading, but it's all ultimately subjective. Still, grades can be useful references when tracking the progression of climbing through the years.

Bibliography

Ain, Morty. "Chris Sharma in his birthday suit," *ESPN The Magazine*. Posted online 9 July, 2013. http://espn.go.com/sports/endurance/story/_/page/bodyissue2013chrissharma/rock-climber-chris-sharma-undresses-2013-body-issue-espn-magazine

"Ashima: Return of the Warrior Ninja Princess." YouTube video, 10:12, Posted by "bigupproductions," November 19, 2012. http://www.youtube.com/watch?v=8-z5XrhrIoQ

Berg, Peter. "The Eagle's Nest," *Alpine Journal* (1995). http://www.alpinejournal.org.uk/Contents/Contents_1995_files/AJ%20 1995%20205-214%20Berg%20Wills.pdf

Bernstein, Jeremy. "Ascending." *The New Yorker*, 31 January 1977. 36

"BD athletes Tommy Caldwell and Kevin Jorgeson attempting to free El Cap's hardest climb – PART ONE." YouTube video, 5:16, Posted by "Black Diamond Equipment," April 13, 2010. http://www.youtube.com/watch?v=t7tWqCwoUUA

"BD athletes Tommy Caldwell and Kevin Jorgeson attempting to free El Cap's hardest climb – PART TWO." YouTube video, 4:00, Posted by "Black Diamond Equipment," April 16, 2010. http://www.youtube.com/watch?v=t3YG86wfnIM

Cahall, Fitz. "Chris Sharma: King of Kings." *Climbing*. http://www.climbing.com/climber/sharma-king-of-kings/

"Chris Sharma, World's First 5.15." YouTube video, 16:31, Posted by "bigupproductions," May 11, 2012. http://www.youtube.com/watch?v=_eTxQLfIUNY

Clark, W.E. LeGros. *History of Primates*. Chicago: Phoenix Books; University of Chicago Press, 1963. 23-49, 92-94.

Dent, C.T. *Mountaineering In The 1800s - The Correct Equipment And Outfit.* Read Country Books, 2010.

Downes, Stephen M. "Are You Experienced," in *Climbing Philosophy for Everyone*, ed. Stephen E. Schmid. Oxford: Wiley-Blackwell, 2010. 197.

Duane, Daniel. "The Revolution Starts at the Bottom." *Sierra Magazine.* http://vault.sierraclub.org/sierra/200403/interview.asp

Emerson, Ralph Waldo. "Uses of Great Men," in *Great Essays*, ed. Houston Peterson. New York: Washington Square Press, 1953. 175-192.

Gill, John. "John Gill's Website." *http:www.johngill.net/*

Goddard, Dale and Udo Neumann. *Performance Rock Climbing.* Mechanicsburg, Pennsylvania: Stackpole Books, 1993.

Heinrich, Bernd. *Why We Run.* New York: Harper Perennial, 2002.

Kelly, Brigit Pegeen. "Pipistrelles," *Song*. Rochester: BOA Editions, Ltd., 1995.

Kotler, Steven. *The Rise of Superman: Decoding the Science of Ultimate Human Performance*. New York: New Harvest, 2014.

Kraft, T.S., et al., "A Natural history of human tree climbing," *Journal of Human Evolution* (2014), http://dx.doi.org/10.1016/j.jhevol.2014.02.002

Kraft, T.S., et al., "Tree Climbing and human evolution," Proceedings of the National Academy of Sciences of the United States of America (2012), www.pnas.org/cgi/doi/10.1073/pnas.1208717110

"Lynn Hill free climb the nose, rare Footage." YouTube video, 1:42, Posted by "jafa340," August 2, 2009. http://www.youtube.com/watch?v=2KlA77j6xAc

Mazel, David, ed. *Mountaineering Women: Stories by Early Climbers.* College Station, Texas: Texas A&M University Press, 1994.

Mermier, Christine M., et al., "Physiological and anthropometric determinants of sport climbing performance," *British Journal of Sports Medicine*, no. 34 (2000): 359-366.

Roberts, David. *Moments of Doubt.* Seattle: The Mountaineers, 1986. Introduction xv-xvi, 237.

Roper, Steve. *Camp 4.* Seattle: The Mountaineers, 1994. 12-13, 15.

Sanzaro, Francis. *The Boulder.* Glasgow: Stone Country Press, 2013. 112, 125.

"Sasha DiGiulian: World #1 on Pure Imagination 5.14d [Official HD Video] presented by adidas." YouTube video, 8:17, Posted by "GearCoop," 18 January, 2012. http://www.youtube.com/watch?v=rM9Btf-Ioos

Sassoon, Donald, *The Culture of the Europeans.* Bercker, Germany; Harper Press, 2006, 7, 56, 330.

"Sean McColl – Dreamcatcher." YouTube video, 3:57, Posted by "Sean McColl," February 23, 2011. http://www.youtube.com/watch?v=8cFdX1ypCXA

Snider, Burr. "The Life of Warren 'Batso' Harding." *Climbing.* http://www.climbing.com/climber/the-life-of-warren-andquot-bat-soandquot-harding/

Swan, Eric. "Zen and the Art of Climbing," in *Climbing Philosophy for Everyone*, ed. Stephen E. Schmid. Oxford: Wiley-Blackwell, 2010. 117-129.

Tallett, Frank. *War and Society in Early-Modern Europe.* New York: Routledge, 1992. 9.

Tejada-Flores, Lito. "Games Climbers Play," *Ascent: Sierra Club Mountaineering Journal*, May 1967.

"Three Weeks & a Day climbing video." YouTube video, 4:27, Posted by "bombsville," September 10, 2008. http://www.youtube. com/watch?v=r2xsu5KDaRw

Todd, Mabel E. *The Thinking Body*. Princeton: Dance Horizons Books, 1937. 6-14, 17, 143, 147.

Weidner, Chris. "For climbing's indoor champions, will the great outdoors become irrelevant?" *Daily Camera*. http://www.dai-lycamera.com/get-out/ci_25226605/chris-weidner-climbings-indoor-champions-will-great-outdoors

Weisner-Hanks, Merry E. *Early Modern Europe*, 1450-1789. New York: Cambridge University Press, 2006. 57.

"What the New NPS Wilderness Climbing Policy Means for Climbers and Bolting," *Vertical Times*, Volume 97, Summer 2013.

William L. Langer, *Political and Social Upheaval – 1832-1852*. New York: Harper Torchbooks, 1969. 534-544.

Wilson, Ken, ed. *The Games Climbers Play*. London: Diadem Books, 1978.

"Wolfgang GULLICH vs Patrick EDLINGER, 1989." YouTube video, 5:53, Posted by "Umberto Tilomelli," July 29, 2009. http://www. youtube.com/watch?v=RaBuNFl1mJM

Index

Acknowledgments

I am indebted to Mike Reardon and Ground Up Publishing for believing in this book. Thank you to Bill, Vicki and Will Burgman, and much appreciation to the rest of my family for the support. Thank you also to Jon Ellison, Arno Ilgner, Francis Sanzaro, John Stewart Watson, Sooyeon Seong, Inkyeong Kim, Gilsoo Yoon, the great crew at Cruxcrush. com, Zach Kling, Sue Song, Ben Cake and Becky Toney. Thank you to Robert Davidson for some valuable revision tips. I am appreciative of the assistance provided by Jaewon Kwon, Doug and Sukja Hansen, Jooey Kim and family and the Chung family. I am grateful to all the friends, specialists, organizations and photographers cited in this book. Finally, I have the deepest gratitude for Dan Kojetin and Zooey Ahn—they were with me on the rocks, and they made the summer of climbing unforgettable.

About the Author

John Burgman is a former editor at *Outdoor Life* and a former Fulbright grant recipient. His writing has appeared online or in print at *Esquire.com, Portland Review, The Rumpus, Crux Crush, Boundary Waters Journal* and other outlets.

Quality books on climbing, built from the ground up

www.GroundUpPublishing.com